How To Measure A

Rainbow

Curtis K. Shelburne

Curtis Shelburne Eph 3:14-21

How To Measure A Rainbow

COVENANT
PUBLISHING

Celebrating the Colors of God's Love

P.O. Box 390 · Webb City, Missouri 64870
Call toll free at 877.673.1015

DEDICATION

With love and appreciation
for
G. B. Shelburne, Jr.
(1913-2000)
&
Wilma Jean Key Shelburne
(1915-1992)

Mom taught me to love God,
to love the stories in God's word,
and to love words themselves;
she taught me that love knows no bounds,
that God loves me completely,
and that so did she.
Dad taught me that the truly strong can be truly gentle;
in word and example he taught me
about the love of the best Father of all.
My father's love made it easy
to believe in the Father's love.
May every word in this book
point to the Word Himself and honor
my mother, my father,
and my Father.

Table of Contents

1. "I Choose You!"   19
Ephesians 1:1-14

Do you remember standing in line as a kid in Phys. Ed. class while the team captains picked their teams? Remember waiting and praying not to be picked last? Good news! God's Kingdom is not like that. In God's economy, he'll pick you in the very first round!

2. Enlightened Eyes   37
Ephesians 1:15-23

God has done amazing things for his people, but sometimes we're like the nearsighted third grader straining to see the blackboard. We need God's vision correction, "enlightened eyes," to open our spirits to the wonder of what God has done for us through Jesus Christ.

3. The Post Office, the Pharisees, and Lazarus   55
Ephesians 2:1-10

Legalism is dead and sterile, whether you're applying it to dead letters or to dead, unproductive religion. Real life and real joy comes only through the mercy and grace of God, through his Son, as an undeserved gift.

4. A Hole in the Wall   75
Ephesians 2:11-22

What I really needed in my study one day was a hole in the wall, but I found out pretty quickly that I needed an expert to punch the hole in exactly the right place. Jesus Christ is the Expert whose love tears down the walls we build between ourselves and our God, and between ourselves and our fellow men and women.

Acknowledgments

Writing a book is a lot like taking a journey, and no traveler gets very far without lots of help. My sincere thanks to:

The 16th & D Church, Muleshoe. Thanks for letting me fill your ears with words about the Word for over sixteen years now. It's been a privilege.

Our larger very small community. Making a Mule of myself has been a pleasure.

John Ketchersid, Lyndon Latham, Jerry Reeves, Robert Lee, Mike Gibson, and David Langford. When we're together you rarely let me sleep but you always make me think.

Steve Cable and Covenant Publishing. A writer without a publisher is like a sailor without a ship. Thanks for the chance to sail with you!

Max Lucado. Thanks for letting God use you to open eyes like mine to new and more beautiful colors in the rainbow of God's love. I'm not at all in your league as a word-crafter, but I'm better for having spent time with you.

Tom Williams. I'm in awe of both your ability to paint with paint and your ability to paint with words. Thanks for encouraging this sailor in search of a ship.

David Key, my uncle. Thanks for reading the Robert Lee, Texas, chapters and for the smiling review: "I only went to sleep once." (You *were* smiling, weren't you?) Two words from you—"It's good"—were a two-note symphony of encouragement to my ears.

B and Gene, my older brothers. Your influence in my life, my thought, and this book is inestimable. Thanks for blazing the trail!

Jim, my younger brother. Writing this has reminded me of how much trouble you've gotten me into down through the years. Hmm. It's been fun, hasn't it? Well, Jacob, thanks for being there. Yours truly, Esau. (Don't carry that analogy too far.)

By the way, I still say you three are lousy shots with *bois d'arc apples*, and you all married way above yourselves!

Ruthie, my sister. Thanks for your encouragement and love. You've been a one-woman cheering section for me for, well, for always. Thanks for your encouragement in this project.

Gene, my brother who is also my editor. Working with words together with you for years has been a real blessing. Your skill in knowing when and where and why and how to make small changes for large effect is no small thing. Thanks!

J. D. and Vernell Nance, my father- and mother-in-law. You two are dear to the heart of God and to mine. Thanks for your love, and for making the trip to Washington fun!

Christopher, Jeffrey, Stephan, and Joshua, my sons. Amazing grace indeed! I'm not sure what surprises me more—that God claims me as a son or that he's allowed me to claim sons like you.

My wife Juana. I thank God for you! Your love and support has been as unfailing as each day's sunrise and even more certain than my next breath. Happy 25th! We married far too young (note that, my sons), but I don't know any husband who married better!

And, not least, for you, the reader: I'm glad you're traveling with me as together we look for rainbows and thrill to the wonderful colors of God's love. The Artist who splashed his sky-canvas with rainbows is the Creator gracing us with the eyes we need to see them.

Let's start looking!

Introduction

"I have set my rainbow in the clouds,
and it will be the sign of the covenant
between me and the earth"
GENESIS 9:13

I wonder how many rainbows the average person living on this globe gets to see in an average lifetime?

I wonder how many folks have really made much of a serious attempt to reach that fabled pot of gold? You know, the one at the end of the rainbow!

And I wonder how old Noah felt when he looked up into the sky the first time after the Flood and saw God's beautiful bow stretching from one end to the other? Noah had seen "up close and personal" the effects of sin. He knew beyond any doubt that sin leads to death.

But Noah also knew better than just about anyone else who has ever lived that God is the God of life. And whenever a rainbow appeared in the sky, Noah back-tracked in his mind to that special day when this Flood-washed world was barely dried out, when the smoke from his post-Flood sacrifice was still lingering in the air, and when God himself appeared.

"Noah," the Almighty had said, "I'm making an agreement with you. I promise that I'll never again destroy earth's life by the waters of a flood. That's my promise to you, to all your descendants, and to all living creatures. And I want this legal! I've told you all about the contract, the promise from me to you, and now I'm ready to sign. Look! Do you see my rainbow splashing color across the sky? Every time you look up and see that bow shimmering with color you're seeing my signature on the dotted line: 'I, Jehovah God, do herewith henceforth and forevermore renounce and disclaim any subsequent intention to again destroy the earth and annihilate its inhabitants by means of the act of God in any way similar to or reminiscent of that act most usually termed and designated as the great Flood.'"

I wonder if Noah wondered if God had forgotten to bring up Noah's part in the covenant?

I wonder if Noah wondered if God had forgotten to bring the form for him to sign?

I wonder if Noah wondered if God had a boatload of angelic lawyers (wouldn't *that* be something!—just kidding) ready to arrive on the scene and disembark from another boat?

This is the first formal covenant we read about in Scripture, and, as one of my favorite writers Philip Yancey has somewhere pointed out, it's just about as basic an agreement as you'll ever find. The party of the first part agrees not to liquidate the party of the second part.

What Noah couldn't completely understand, but what God was saying to old Noah, and to you and me, is this: "It is not my will to destroy the earth; it is my will to redeem it."

When you look up into the sky following a life-giving rain and see a rainbow, you're looking at the love of God stretching out as far as the east is from the west. You're looking at the beautiful symbol of an even more beautiful promise.

But if you want to see an even more impressive proof of God's love, I'd suggest you focus on another symbol that points to an even greater covenant and an even better promise.

Let the rainbow point you to the cross.

Look at the cross of Christ.

That cross points to a new covenant ratified by the blood of

God's own Son, the blood that was "poured out for many for the forgiveness of sins" (Matthew 26:28).

Peter was pointing to the cross and its power when he wrote, "For Christ died for sins once for all, the righteous for the unrighteous, to bring you to God" (1 Peter 3:18).

The Son of God has the cross in mind when he says to you and to me, sons of Adam and daughters of Eve deserving of death not only because of our First Parents' sin but also because of our own, "I'll pay the price. I'll die in your stead."

Because of the cross, God's Son can say to debtors like us hopelessly in debt and doomed to be forever enslaved, "You're free. What's more, you're rich because my riches are yours. I'll pay the price for your sin. I'll become your redemption."

Because of a cross, Jesus can remind religious Pharisees like me whose pride is their poison, who are tempted to rise up and say, "I'll get my salvation the old-fashioned way; I'll earn it," that the old-fashioned way was never good enough, that the only way to lay claim to this most precious pearl is to open my hands to receive it as a gift, and that the new covenant is precisely this—that the only thing I'm really capable of giving is the only thing for which he asks. My faith. My trust. My love.

And because of a cross, as I fall at his feet, laying aside the filthy garments of my pride, haughty robes that have so often tripped me up, the Father justifies me "freely by his grace through the redemption that came by Christ Jesus" (Romans 3:24).

And I'm a little like I suspect Noah might have been.

Lord, what's the catch? I want to know. What do I have to sign?

No catch, he replies. Just give me all of your love. On a cross, I gave you all of mine.

Two beautiful symbols of two wonderful covenants.

The rainbow and the cross.

Folks in my part of the country have been a little short on rainbows for the past several years. That's because we've been more than a little short on rain!

You remember? The wet stuff? "Water falling in drops condensed from vapor in the atmosphere." Rain.

People around here have had times when they almost forgot what it looks like, smells like, feels like. But it's absolutely wonderful.

To a thirsty land—parched, dry, and slowly burning up—relief is spelled R-A-I-N.

I love the smell of rain. It smells clean and fresh, and every breath of rain-kissed air seems to fill us up with new hope and renewed possibilities for life and growth. The smell of rain is the smell of life.

Sometimes when it has been so long since we smelled something that beautiful we almost begin to think and act and live—

      as if rivers were made only to hold dust and sand,
    as if any recollection of cool rejuvenation was just delirium
       brought on by the unrelenting heat,
    as if all our hopes were really meant to be just as dead and
       dry and brown as the scorched and dying ground
          stretched out around us.

People who have been living in drought conditions long enough all too easily begin to believe that drought is all there is and that words like "cool" and "wet" and "green" were just figments of our imaginations anyway. Maybe they were proper dreams for children, but adults living in the real world should know better. Drought, we too easily begin to think, is all there is. Deal with it.

And so we let the heat scorch our dreams as it plays havoc with our senses.

A world that is just brown is a world without much color. And, I suppose, if we've not seen anything beautiful for a very long time or if our sight is so drought-stricken that we've lost the ability to recognize beauty when we do see it, our eyes begin to expect to see nothing of beauty. We become like people who have all sorts of money to buy wonderful food but who've lost the ability to taste it.

But then, thank God, the rain comes!

Every breath fills us with the smell of life. God breathes his hope into our hearts and reminds us that the death we've been smelling so long that we thought it was all there is?—well, that is not all there is.

Not even close.

And, rejuvenated, we look up, and there, shining across the newly-washed and crystal clear sky, catching us completely by surprise with the depth of its beauty and the richness of its color, is a rainbow, a precious gift straight from the hand of God.

That gift is almost better than the rain, and, like the rain, it's a precious gift because it *is* a gift. Rain doesn't come just because you think it's a good time to water the lawn. Or even when you know for sure it's a good time to water your crop. And it's pretty hard to just order up a rainbow for evening viewing whenever you please.

Rainbows are gifts of God's grace.

And, like God's grace, part of their glory is that they catch us by surprise.

But if we know where to look, and if we work to keep our eyes open, I'm convinced we can thrill to the most glorious rainbow of all pretty much anytime at all.

It's the rainbow of God's love.

It's the multicolored and magnificent expression of his mercy and grace.

It's the color of his joy and the panorama of his love.

I love rainbows, and seeing one is worth some trouble. That's why my personal policy regarding rainbows is that I'll rise from even the most sumptuous meal, the most comfortable chair, or the loveliest nap to take a trip outside to just get a look at one.

And now, I've got another trip in mind.

And I need a companion for the journey,

a friend for the road,

a fellow-traveler for fellowship on the tour.

And I know where I'd like to go.

The trip I've got in mind is a trip right through the Apostle Paul's beautiful words to the Ephesians.

I must confess, I'm not completely sure what we'll find there. Our Guide has been known to sometimes lead travelers in some directions they hadn't planned to go!

But I'm sure of this. No Guide has ever loved his travelers more, and whatever we find along the road will be wonderful.

You see, if rainbows are shimmering and brilliant expressions of God's love, well, Paul's *Letter to the Ephesians* is a rainbow-rich environment!

I'd be honored if you'd come along with me.

Let's take a wonderful trip.

Let's look for some rainbows!

Chapter 1

Paul, an apostle of Christ Jesus by the will of God,
To the saints in Ephesus, the faithful in Christ Jesus:
Grace and peace to you from God our Father and the Lord
Jesus Christ.

Praise be to the God and Father of our Lord Jesus Christ, who
has blessed us in the heavenly realms with every spiritual blessing in Christ. For he chose us in him before the creation of the
world to be holy and blameless in his sight. In love he predestined us to be adopted as his sons through Jesus Christ, in accordance with his pleasure and will—to the praise of his glorious
grace, which he has freely given us in the One he loves. In him
we have redemption through his blood, the forgiveness of sins,
in accordance with the riches of God's grace that he lavished on
us with all wisdom and understanding. And he made known to
us the mystery of his will according to his good pleasure, which
he purposed in Christ, to be put into effect when the times will
have reached their fulfillment—to bring all things in heaven and
on earth together under one head, even Christ.

In him we were also chosen, having been predestined
according to the plan of him who works out everything in
conformity with the purpose of his will, in order that we, who
were the first to hope in Christ, might be for the praise of his
glory. And you also were included in Christ when you heard the
word of truth, the gospel of your salvation. Having believed, you
were marked in him with a seal, the promised Holy Spirit, who is
a deposit guaranteeing our inheritance until the redemption of
those who are God's possession—to the praise of his glory.

Ephesians 1:1-14

"I Choose You!"

For he chose us in him
before the creation of the world. . . .
In him we were also chosen, . . .
EPHESIANS 1:4, 11

The sun was hot and the little ten-year-old boy standing on the edge of the playground could feel the sweat running down his back. He was one human slat in the long fence-line of some twenty other ten-year-old boys—potential players for that day's P.E. soccer teams.

Soccer was okay. He didn't mind soccer. To be very honest, it was P.E. he had a problem with. To be even more honest, it was the brain-dead P.E. coach he had a problem with.[1]

The boy knew he was supposed to be respectful and obedient, and he tried hard. And really he was. But inside he wondered if the guy remembered beans about being a kid.

Had *he* ever stood on the sidelines scared spitless that he might be the one who did something the rest of the class made fun of that day?

Had *he* ever stood in a line-up praying there would be no "skins and shirts" games today that would force him to peel and reveal once more the fact that, compared to Arnold Schwarzenegger, he was about as big and muscular as a goosebump on one of Arnold's biceps? Had the coach ever stood there topless looking like a lily-white wimp—white except for the billboard-red embarrassment painted across his face? Probably not.

How to Measure a Rainbow

On a good day, from the boy's perspective, the man could make P.E. only moderately humiliating. On a bad day . . . ?

On a bad day they stood in lines just like the one he was standing in right now, waiting to be absolutely and utterly humiliated.

It was record-setting hot. But that wasn't the main reason his mouth was dry and he felt half sick. It was what was happening. Again.

The coach had blown the whistle to form up the line, and he was asking the assembled inmates to choose who they wanted to be team captains. It'd take two, and they were quickly picked.

One was Mr. Popularity. The class always picked him first. For everything. The other was the class bully. You always picked him right close to the top of the heap, too, because he'd beat the tar out of you if you didn't!

The two team captains swaggered out to the front. They flipped a coin to see who would go first, and the serious business of humiliation got underway.

One after another, the boys were picked for each team, and the crop of candidates poised on the field shriveled and shrank as the most athletic were harvested first. The lucky few whose self-esteem was already well-established got another gratuitous dose of affirmation as they went in the first few rounds.

But the boys who couldn't buy self-esteem on a bet lost a little bit more of the little they had as they stood on the auction block. It's bad enough to be a slave, but to be a slave nobody will buy is unspeakably worse!

More sweat, running like a salty river filling full the pool of his embarrassment, coursed its way down the little boy's back.

The bidding was slower now. He wasn't the only one with head down diligently inspecting his shoe laces, kicking at crab grass, and praying to go in the next round. The captains were posturing carefully to at least avoid getting stuck with the worst liabilities.

And then the unenthusiastic nod of the head, the wag of the finger, and the mumbled "You!" ended the day's ordeal.

It could have been worse. He could have been the poor kid who was dead last.

He'd pick up some bruises on his shins from today's game, but he didn't mind those. He could kick back! The bruises to his shaky ego *before* the game were the ones that hurt.

Besides that, he could look on the bright side. He might have a way out.

Fungus.

Yeah, fungus.

He had a friend who got a plantar's wart on his foot and got to skip P.E. and work in the library for a whole six weeks. They don't have "skins and shirts" in the library. And no one there picks teams.

Do you recall living through the kind of scene I've just tried to paint for you? I hope you don't, but I'll bet you do.

Even if you can't remember ever enduring this kind of humiliation as a child, I'll bet you could identify with the little fellow in the story because the fear he encountered is, sadly, not a fear that automatically disappears when we trade puppy dog tails for "9 to 5" jobs.

Adults, too, know the fear of not fitting in. Of being the odd man (or woman) out. Of being the fifth wheel. Of being a square peg when everyone else seems to be fitting very nicely into round holes.

Oh, yes, adults know that fear, too.

The new couple in the community feel it when they go

through the buffet line for the first "his and hers" banquet at the civic club, start a new table, and no one sits with them.

The retirement-age professor in the university department feels it when he stumbles time and again onto informal gatherings of younger, more "cutting edge" scholars, who would never be so discourteous as to actively exclude him from their conversations, but just as surely would never make much effort to bring him in.

The middle-aged woman at work feels it the moment she walks into a buzzing break room for coffee with her peers, and the "buzz" ceases the moment she steps through the door.

The nauseating flush made up of one part embarrassment and two parts fear could come on the job, at the office, at the club, in the meeting, or on the pew. But you recognize it when it comes.

It's the fear of not being chosen. On an even deeper level, it's the fear of not being *worth* choosing.

And we've all felt it.

We've all felt it, and we've had to decide, consciously or not, what to do about it.

I think we'll be happier if we make some very conscious decisions as to how to handle this "fifth-wheel" fear, this fear of not fitting in, of not being chosen, of not being worth choosing.

I suppose the specific ways people try to deal with the fear of not being chosen are as different and varied as the folks feeling the fear, but I think I've recognized some of the coping mechanisms they use. Most of us have used them ourselves from time to time.

The "Let's Build a Callus" Approach

Some people try to build calluses at the same time as they build walls, calluses to deaden the pain, walls to keep the realization they fear from scaling the limits of their lives once again.

I once watched a haunting made-for-television movie, all the more disturbing because it was based on a true story, about a minister (a pastor who displayed far more courage than I ever could) and his amazing wife who took in a little girl and her even smaller brother as foster children and then decided to adopt them permanently.

I've long since forgotten the name and most of the specific circumstances of the show, but I remember distinctly that "accidents" began to happen. As hard as it was for them to believe, the couple finally began to notice that people who stayed around the little girl for long got hurt. Other children were not safe around her. Nor was anyone else. Her own little brother and, later, the adoptive mother, she almost killed before they discovered what she was doing and why.

This tormented little girl had never in her entire life felt really loved or chosen. Her own mother had rejected her. And every time she began to get close to foster parents, for one reason or another she was moved to another set.

They didn't intend to hurt her. Reject her. Destroy her already almost nonexistent sense of worth. But they did.

And so, in her terribly twisted mind, she made the cold calculation that she would never again let anyone hurt her. She'd hurt them first.

And she did.

Most people don't go quite that far, but lots of folks use basically the same logic. You see them in families. In businesses. And, yes, in churches.

Unlike the disturbed little girl in that disturbing movie, they'd never hurt anyone else physically, but, using the very same logic she used, they hurt themselves by resolving to keep their distance, come what may, from anyone who ever tries to get really close.

Somewhere, sometime, somehow they got hurt. For some reason, they've felt (with good reason or not, in reality or maybe just in perception; it doesn't matter because they feel it just the same) the sting of rejection, and, consciously or not, they've determined that it won't happen again.

They look the same as anyone else.

They'll smile and shake your hand. They'll exchange pleasantries and talk about the weather.

But they won't let you get too close. Not again. They won't open themselves again to the hurt of what they perceived as rejection.

Oh, they still come to family reunions. Or go to work. And maybe they still come to church. But there's a big part of themselves they're holding back. Trying to shield themselves from the pain of rejection, they end up insulating themselves from the comfort of love.

Emotional calluses work all too well. If we use them to keep from being burned by pain, to some extent, they'll work. But we'll find they also filter out the warmth of love.

The "Round Is Wrong/Square Is Right" Approach

Some people cope with perceived rejection—with the fear of not being chosen, not being worth choosing—by taking a more active approach to the problem.

They're treated like square pegs in a round-hole world? They'll set out to prove to themselves and everyone around them that round is wrong and square is right.

At church, they may try to back it up with Scripture. They'll out-Pharisee the Pharisees. Do-it-yourself, law-centered religion makes a very fine tool for this sort of thing.

At work, they may try to fade into the woodwork, but just as likely they may work harder, longer, more feverishly than anyone else on the job. Not feeling that who they are is good enough, they're even more likely than the rest of us to look to their jobs for the sense of identity and worth they haven't acquired elsewhere.

At school, they may just sit on the sidelines, but just as likely they may academically and/or even athletically beat the daylights out of anyone in sight.

You see, people who want desperately to run with the pack but haven't been allowed to join it may decide to run by themselves—way out in front. They'll get out in front by sheer determination borne out of a deep need to "win."

Some of these "competitors" try to get to the front of the bunch by stinging the others around them. One of the most tempting of all sins for any of us is gossip, but it is never more tempting than when we feel a desperate need to slow down the people we perceive as competitors. If we feel a desperate need to get to the top of the heap, we seem to know instinctively (it's a tribute to our fallen nature) that one effective though pernicious way to get there is to climb over the bodies of colleagues who are dazed by poison from our tongues. As Morris Mandel writes, "Gossip is the most deadly microbe. It has neither legs nor wings. It is composed entirely of tales, and most of them have stings."[2]

The highly-charged I'll-beat-the-daylights-out-of-you-in-any-area-you-choose spirit of people who cope by competing is a sad kind of insulation. It insulates them from the truth that they'd really give everything they've accomplished, everything they've "won," just to fit in with the folks they've beaten.

They're square pegs in a round-hole world.

They've got to prove that square is better.

One thing's sure. It's lonelier.

The "Suck the Life Out of Others" Approach

Some people become so hungry for affection that they devour the very ones who try to give it.

How to Measure a Rainbow

As a young would-be minister having just moved into a new city, newly married, newly enrolled in school, I was beginning part-time "intern" work as a youth minister, etc. (the "etc." was by far the biggest part of the job!), with a church in that area when I met a young member of the church who was probably not more than 20 himself. I'll call him Bob.

Bob was intelligent. He was talented.

But he was also, I discovered very quickly, absolutely starved for human affection.

You never saw a starving, belly-distended, African hunger relief poster child any hungrier for food than poor Bob was for some simple affection, the kind that would tell him that, with one person at least, he fit in.

But because his every word telegraphed so loudly his deep need for love, because his every action advertised his need for acceptance just as surely and obviously as if the message were painted across his forehead in red, he pushed away the very thing he needed the most, and he virtually assured that he would never get it.

I tried to give it.

I tried to be nice to him. That, after all, seemed like the Christian thing to do. And he wasn't at all a bad guy. I thought I could at least be his friend.

But he wouldn't let me.

It wasn't that he didn't want friendship. No, indeed.

The problem again was that he needed acceptance so badly that it became for him an absolute craving, a fierce hunger, and he completely devoured those who tried to give it.

I started out by simply being nice to him, and it was exactly as if I'd patted a dog starved for affection. Once thus encouraged, he slobbered and drooled and sucked the life out of me so voraciously that the only way to retain any personal space at all was to be almost cruelly blunt.

I Choose you!

And so, in a thousand ways we who feel so desperately the need to be chosen, the need to know we're worth choosing, try to cope.

Some gossip.

Some become workaholics.

Some become pathologically competitive.

Some almost beg for love and acceptance.

How Can We Get the Acceptance We Need?

How do we ever get it? Is it ever possible to get over the fear of not being chosen, the fear of not being worth choosing, the fear that if grownups lined up to choose teams we'd be chosen dead last?

I think it is.

If this sort of fear is beginning to control our lives we need to realize that everyone has dealt to some extent with the very same fear.

We need to recognize that our feelings aren't always accurate. Some of us have days when, for whatever reason, we're so insecure that if we saw a football huddle, we'd be sure those fellows were talking about us!

And we'd be wrong!

It may be that the lady in your Bible study group that you thought was becoming a close friend really was a bit cool to you on Thursday, but do you have to jump to the conclusion that she's rejecting your friendship?

Boy, it surely seemed that the boss breezed through your office yesterday and hardly spoke at all, much less made any comment on the extra hours you put in over the weekend, but does that really mean that he's upset with you, and your next evaluation will be low, and your next pay raise nonexistent?

And so what if a few of the couples at church got together

and you don't even remember being invited? Does that necessarily mean the worst—that they've gotten together and decided they don't want you around?

Do you want to absolutely insure that you'll be unhappy and miserable?

One of the best ways to get that done is to spend lots of time attributing the worst possible motives to other people's actions and taking the slightest word or movement or expression absolutely personally.

Want to be unhappy?

Make yourself and your feelings the center of your universe. To be totally subjective, overly emotional, less than rational, and to interpret everything that others do or say as their estimate of your personal worth is to be absolutely miserable most of the time.

It is also, by the way, to be mistaken most of the time.

Mrs. Smith's grimace may not mean she hates my sermon. It may simply mean she has gas.

If you must make a guess as to the reason behind someone else's words, motives, or mood, choose the more positive one and you'll be right more often than you'll be wrong.

You'll also be a great deal happier.

Worried about not being chosen? About not being worth choosing?

Realize that you're not alone, that some feel it even more acutely than you do.

Then resolve that no matter how far down the draft pick you are yourself, when your turn comes to choose, you're picking the little guy first!

The best way to insure that you'll never fit in at work, home, church, or school is to spend lots of time worrying about not fitting in. Try worrying instead about someone else who seems to be always on the outside looking in.

I Choose you!

And then you'll be sure to hear on one wonderful day, "Well done, good and faithful servant! I tell you the truth, whatever you've done for one of the least of these brothers of mine, you've done for me."[3]

Jesus said that about cups of cold water and visits to the sick and imprisoned. Affirming others as people of worth is surely a kindness that fits well in the same category!

Want to get over the fear of not being chosen, of not being worth choosing? I've saved the most important counsel for last. It's wisdom that comes from the Apostle Paul, and, I firmly believe, from the Holy Spirit himself.

The Most Important Advice

In Ephesians 1 Paul deals with this whole subject in two ways. First, he says, you're worried about not being chosen? You're worried about not being worth choosing?

Don't worry. You can know for sure.

You're not worth choosing.

You're really not.

Not if worth only accrues by means of meritorious performance or outstanding achievement.

The world may talk about what a person is worth in terms of her balance sheet and the assets he's managed to accumulate by brute force or power of intellect.

But don't expect God to.

Our intellects are not particularly impressive to the One who crafted everything from the inner workings of the grasshopper to the moons of Jupiter.

Don't expect our human strength to bring any gasps of awe from the Creator who painted the Milky Way and set the oceans and tides in motion.

And do we suppose in our vanity and pride that our feeble

29

attempts at goodness could ever put God in our debt for even a moment?

If we could keep every one of the commandments perfectly all of our lives long we still would be doing only what is required.

Nothing more.

And the truth is, we don't even come close to keeping all the commandments. If we claim we do, we've just broken the one about not "bearing false witness" (Exodus 20:16).

No. Sorry. There is no question about our being "worth choosing" if worth has to come from our side of the equation.

But thank God it does not!

The Best News of All

What Paul tells us, secondly, is one of the greatest, most beautiful, most amazing pieces of good news this world has ever heard. It is foundational to the good news of the Gospel itself.

It's such good news that the great apostle can hardly contain himself. Like the messenger standing at the door waiting to tell the couple who answer that they've won the Publisher's Clearinghouse Sweepstakes, Paul can hardly wait to give us this news.

He's so excited that in his *Letter to the Ephesians* he barely gets past "Dear Ephesians" before he absolutely erupts into a cascading torrent of praise!

"Praise be to the God and Father of our Lord Jesus Christ for giving us through Christ every possible spiritual benefit as citizens of Heaven!" (1:3, PHILLIPS).

And then, to each of us standing in line in this world with butterflies in our stomachs,

I Choose you!

        studying our shoelaces,
                kicking at crab grass—
to each of us hoping against hope that before we get to the very last round and we're picked only because the rules say we have to be—

to each us of who've worked ourselves to the bone trying to pathetically prove that we have some value, trying to convince ourselves and just maybe somebody else that at least we wouldn't be a complete detriment if they'd just please, please pick us for their team—

to each of us, the greatest Captain of all says,

I choose you!

Not because I have to, not because someone made me, not because of any ulterior motive, not because I'm impressed with your batting average.

Simply out of who I am.

I choose you!

To bathe you in my grace.

To enfold you in my mercy.

To give you new life with my love.

And that, my friends, is the Gospel, the Good News, that Paul can hardly wait to tell the Ephesians, that the Holy Spirit rushes to announce to our hearts right now.

To people who are afraid they might not be chosen.

To people afraid they might not be worth choosing.

To you. To me.

The Holy Spirit of God says, "I choose you!"

For he chose us in him before the creation of the world to be holy and blameless in his sight. In love he predestined us to be adopted as his sons through Jesus Christ, in accordance with his pleasure and will—to the praise of his glorious grace, which he has freely given us in the One he loves. In him we have redemption through his blood, the forgiveness of sins. . . . In him we were also chosen, . . . in order that we, who were the first to

31

hope in Christ, might be for the praise of his glory. And you also were included in Christ when you heard the word of truth, the gospel of your salvation. Having believed, you were marked in him with a seal, the promised Holy Spirit, who is a deposit guaranteeing our inheritance until the redemption of those who are God's possession—to the praise of his glory"

(Ephesians 1:4-7a, 11-14).

If you think you're a fifth wheel in God's economy, think again.

You don't have to worry about whether or not you fit in.

You don't have to compete with the rest of the team because we're all chosen on the very same basis.

His mercy.

His love.

His grace.

And so, may I share with you right now the best news of all, the message of the Gospel?

God chooses you!

And, wonder of wonders, he chose you in the first round!

In that knowledge, now you can go play the game of life knowing beyond any shadow of a doubt that you've been chosen to wear the colors of the King.

He chooses *you*!

I Choose you!

That God Would Choose Me

❀

That God would choose me
   stretches the bounds of sanity.

"Jesus loves me, this I know,"
   but so much?
     so well?
      so deeply?
       so . . . ?
Why, oh, why, should he love me so?
   But, lo,
     He did,
      He died,
       He does!

One length of life is ne'er enough
   To fathom the depths of that deepest love.
For that most blessed task, miraculously,
   Mortal must indeed put on immortality.

But here and now, presently,
   right here,
    right now,
     directly,
What, I ask, with breath He gave,
   Can I give the Giver? Tell me, pray!

Can I enrich,
     impress,
      indebt,
   the Author of Life
    with the offer of my love?
As well might a baby's breath begin to spin
   The winds that spawn a hurricane! Insane.

But, for Adam's race, even a small step
   in the direction of humility
Is a giant step
   in the direction of sanity.

God chooses man chooses God. Mystery!
   Wonder of wonders, God chooses me.

Chapter 2

For this reason, ever since I heard about your faith in the Lord Jesus and your love for all the saints, I have not stopped giving thanks for you, remembering you in my prayers. I keep asking that the God of our Lord Jesus Christ, the glorious Father, may give you the Spirit of wisdom and revelation, so that you may know him better. I pray also that the eyes of your heart may be enlightened in order that you may know the hope to which he has called you, the riches of his glorious inheritance in the saints, and his incomparably great power for us who believe. That power is like the working of his mighty strength, which he exerted in Christ when he raised him from the dead and seated him at his right hand in the heavenly realms, far above all rule and authority, power and dominion, and every title that can be given, not only in the present age but also in the one to come. And God placed all things under his feet and appointed him to be head over everything for the church, which is his body, the fullness of him who fills everything in every way.

Ephesians 1:15-23

"Enlightened Eyes"

*I pray also that the eyes of your heart
may be enlightened
in order that you may know . . .*
EPHESIANS 1:18

A s I recall, it was only one year after the year I fell in love with my second grade teacher that I fell into hate with our school nurse.

"If only the old band-aid pusher had minded her own business . . ."

With all the indignation a myopic eight-year-old could muster, I muttered something to that effect. In fact, our school nurse was a savvy lady who minded her own business quite well. Her business was to give eye exams to third-graders like me. I should have thanked her. But I was in no mood.

"Why doesn't she go pick on somebody else?"

I was pretty sure I could already see the "hand writing on the wall." (Actually, I couldn't. I couldn't see the big "E" on the eye chart on the wall, either). This meddlesome woman would be calling my parents soon to report that their young son was as blind as the proverbial bat, and that would be the beginning of all manner of trouble.

She did, and it was.

Before the waning of many moons, I became the unhappy owner of a brand new pair of eyeglasses and an enormous load of self-consciousness. I was about to become, I was sure, the first bespectacled spectacle ever to walk down the halls of San Jacinto Elementary School.

Not usually a disobedient child, I felt forced to take drastic action. I would not wear those things! I'd resist for all I was worth! Oh, I'd wear them to school, but then I'd lose them until time to go home.

But I was blind to the fatal flaw in my plan.

You see, the hated spectacles had to be put on at least briefly. When I grudgingly looked through the lenses (encased in very un-cool-looking black & brown swirled plastic frames), I discovered to my utter amazement that the world surely looked good in focus! I hadn't realized what I'd been missing!

Trees had leaves and bark! And the colors? What amazing colors! Colors in focus are a great deal deeper and richer than the blurry blobs of color I'd become accustomed to. The world in focus was a far more exciting place than the world I'd been seeing!

Now, I ask you, did my glasses, ugly as they were, really change the world?

No, but they drastically improved the way I viewed the world. I was suddenly getting the real picture, and it was great! And even though I hated those spectacles, I liked the spectacular world they helped me to see.

I thought of all of this years later when I ran across the title of a book by Edith Schaeffer, *A Way of Seeing.*[1]

A way of seeing. In many respects, that's what Christianity is. It's a way of seeing the people, places, and events that make up the stories of our lives.

For fallen human beings who don't always see the world very clearly, seeing the world through the eyes of Christ opens us up to new and unimaginably beautiful horizons, a kind of clarity we've only dreamed of, some colors we'd long since forgotten, and some deeper and richer hues than any we've ever seen.

"Enlightened Eyes"

Isn't it strange, though, how strongly most of us resist 20/20 vision? Living in what is so often a dark world, we hardly know how to react to the new light and vision offered by Christ. We've been blind to so much beauty and the world has been out of focus for us for so long that when we finally allow the Great Optician—I mean, Physician!—to illumine our lives, we are amazed at the beauty and the wonder of life in focus.

I guess that old school nurse did me a favor, after all. And I'm absolutely sure that Christ did.

When Paul Penned These Words . . .

I don't know what sort of view the Apostle Paul had from his window, or if he had a window at all, when he penned his words to the Christians at Ephesus. I don't know what he could see.

When Paul was writing these words, he was a "prisoner for the Lord," (4:1) an "ambassador in chains" (6:20). Was he in a dark Roman cell locked away from the light?

Probably not. The indication seems to be that Paul wrote this letter while he was under house arrest in Rome. Under arrest? Yes. A prisoner? Yes. In prison? Well, not exactly.

Since he was not a dangerous criminal and not considered dangerously subversive politically, he seems to have been allowed to rent a house in Rome and live by himself, though a soldier was always with him, perhaps even chained to him, as a guard.[2]

So maybe he did have a window, but what I'm most curious about is not what he saw through windows but what he saw through his own eyes. It seems to me that those who argue that Paul's "thorn in the flesh" (2 Corinthians 12:7) could have been an eye problem might well be on to something. Remember how Paul, near the end of his letter to the Galatians, takes up the pen and writes, "See what large letters I use as I write to you with my own hand" (6:11)? As if to say, "Here's how you can know this letter is authentic. You know very well that I write large letters because I have a hard time making out small ones!"

Was Paul's physical view diminished? Were his physical circumstances dominantly dreary? Were his fleshly eyes darkened?

I don't know.

But I do know that few men have ever seen the light more clearly.

Strange.

Who could have dreamed that some of the most beautiful music this world has ever heard would come from the heart and soul of Ludwig van Beethoven after he had gone deaf?

Who would have thought that one of the twentieth century's greatest women of vision would be the blind and deaf Helen Keller?

Who would guess what a powerful life could come from the diminutive form of a physically weak and frail Mother Teresa?

Picture a deafened Beethoven praying that those who hear his symphony may have their ears washed clean with musical joy.

Picture the blind Helen Keller speaking to audiences all over the world to help them see the beauty she sees.

Picture little Mother Teresa on the platform towering above presidents as she urges the strong to remember the weak and thus be truly strong.

And picture Paul imprisoned, Paul perhaps weak in sight but mighty in genuine vision, Paul who gives thanks to God for the Ephesians, Paul who petitions the Father continually that they may know their God better—picture this Paul, his own physical world circumscribed by Roman might and darkened at times within and without, seeing with such beautiful vision that his prayer for the Ephesians is that they, too, may have "the eyes of their heart" enlightened.

"Enlightened Eyes"

For people living in a dark world, enlightened eyes—eyes wide open to the beauty of God's love, able to discern the deep hues of his joy and experience the rich colors of his mercy—spell the difference between light and darkness, hope and despair, clear vision and groping blindness.

When Our Eyes Are Enlightened

If our eyes are enlightened, Paul writes, we will be able to see the hope to which God has called us.

A human being can endure almost anything if he has hope.

You can try to starve him in a Great Depression.

You can lock him up in a Dachau or an Auschwitz.

You can confine him flat of his back in a hospital bed or chain him to a wheelchair and a ventilator.

But you can't defeat him. As long as he has hope.

Jewish psychiatrist Viktor Frankl was one of the millions of Jews oppressed by the Nazis during World War II. As quoted in *Leadership Journal*, Frankl writes that he lost almost everything—property, family, possessions. For years he had been working to complete a book on the importance of finding meaning in life. Before he was arrested, he had hidden the manuscript of that book in the lining of his coat. But when he arrived in Auschwitz, even that was taken from him, and it was a devastating loss. He writes, "I had to undergo and to overcome the loss of my mental child. And now it seemed as if nothing and no one would survive me; neither a physical nor a mental child of my own!"[3]

This man whose most important life's work had been his research on finding meaning in life was now himself being tried by fire. He found himself, as he says in his own words, "confronted with the question whether under such circumstances my life was ultimately void of any meaning."[4] The researcher was now himself the test subject in the crucible of suffering.

The time soon came when the Nazis required their prisoners to give up their clothes. Frankl describes the experience:

> I had to surrender my clothes and in turn inherited the worn-out rags of an inmate who had already been sent to the gas chamber. . . . Instead of the many pages of my manuscript, I found in a pocket of the newly acquired coat one single page torn out of a Hebrew prayer book, containing the most important Jewish prayer, *Shema Yisrael*. ["Hear, O Israel! The Lord our God is one God. And you shall love the Lord your God with all your heart and with all your soul and with all your might."]
>
> How should I have interpreted such a "coincidence" other than as a challenge to *live* my thoughts instead of merely putting them on paper?[5]

Years later, when Viktor Frankl finally published his book, a much different, much more meaningful, book entitled *Man's Search for Meaning*, he would draw deeply on his own experience to write, "There is nothing in the world, I venture to say, that would so effectively help one to survive even the worst conditions as the knowledge that there is a meaning in one's life. There is much wisdom in the words of Nietzsche: 'He who has a *why* to live for can bear almost any *how*.'"[6]

Time and again the truth of those words has been tested in the crucible of suffering and has stood the test.

The Apostle Peter wrote to Christians in the first century, people who were misunderstood, persecuted, and punished in particularly horrid ways during the reign of the mad emperor Nero (and Peter's words are even more poignant when you realize that he himself—and Paul—would perish in that persecution). Peter wrote to people who needed to be reminded of their heavenly hope because their hope for this world was shaky indeed. He wrote to people whose minds needed to be focused on the mercy and love of their heavenly King, people all too well aware of the fiendishness of their earthly emperor. He wrote to people who needed the assurance of an unfading inheritance prepared by their heavenly Father because their earthly security was fading fast.

He wrote to people who needed hope.

If he could just help them see beyond the present trouble . . .

If he could just motivate them to be strong in trying times . . .

If he could just help their eyes to be enlightened so they could catch a glimpse even through the darkness of the riches and love, the mercy and grace, of the God who still loved them and would see them through . . .

If God could use Peter's words to open the eyes of his people to genuine hope, then they could endure.

Today we may not be facing Auschwitz or Nero, but we live in a world where hope is still as precious as light in the darkness and sight to the blind. We know what it means to cry for a child, or lose a mate to death or divorce, or to live in physical or emotional pain. Hitler and Nero are dead, but madness and wickedness live on, and we desperately need hope when we're tempted to despair. When we're walking through difficult and dark chapters of our lives, we need a heavenly Father who can stroke our hair, tuck us in with his love, and tell us the end of the story, that all will one day be well.

The words Peter wrote to our forefathers in the faith are words filled with hope that still outshines the darkness: "Praise be to the God and Father of our Lord Jesus Christ! In his great mercy he has given us new birth into a living hope through the resurrection of Jesus Christ . . ." (1 Peter 1:3).

If our eyes are enlightened, Paul writes to the Ephesians, and to us, we'll be able to see "the riches of his glorious inheritance in the saints" (1:18).

How to Measure a Rainbow

The Words of a Rich Man

You may not know it, but you're reading the words of a rich man. Yes, I'm rich. I just thought I'd let you know that before you read any farther.

But maybe I should also tell you that the riches I'm talking about have nothing to do with money.

Historian Will Durant describes the Romans who lived just before Christ: "Everyone longed for money. Everyone judged or was judged in terms of money."[7] It was a pretty poor yardstick for real wealth then, and it's no better now.

If I ever needed any reminder of how rich I am, it came for me one cool fall evening several years ago in Robert Lee, Texas. My three brothers (ages 38-60!), my 83-year-old father, and one nephew met at Robert Lee at my maternal grandparents' old homeplace, now owned by one brother.

We are all preachers. But for those few days, we were painters, weedeater operators, firepit builders, and hurlers of *bois d'arc* apples! *Bois d'arc* is the name of a tree and means "iron wood" in French. Take my word for it—the fruit is pretty solid, too! I knew those yahoos would hurl some *bois d'arc* apples my way, but men of the cloth have big voices and lousy arms. I figured I was safe, as long as they were aiming at me; it was the blind-hurl approach that really worried me!

I dislike painting so much that I tore through a couple of hundred yards of weedeater line to avoid it, occasionally lugging the smoking weedeater past my paintbrush-wielding siblings so I could reload and mutter, "You ain't a power tool operator, you ain't diddly!", re-fuel, and fire up again. But I ran out of weeds. Rather than stoop to painting, I dug a ditch and built a stone-lined firepit.

We used to have grand bonfires before Robert Lee, of all places, modernized and passed a "no burning" ordinance. Now we need a pit and a token Oscar Meyer tube steak to be legal.

"Enlightened Eyes"

So I built the pit.

That night, we sat around a fine fire, and my father, always a ceremonial sort, announced, "Fellows, I want to make a speech." Shorter than the speech old Moses delivered in Deuteronomy just before his people were to enter the Promised Land, it was, to me, no less moving. The patriarch of our clan, the man who gave us life and love and leadership, the strongest, gentlest man I have ever known, simply told us how proud he was of us and what we are doing. He gave us, I suppose you could say, his blessing.

My grandparents, both sides, were not wealthy people. My dad was an amazingly fine money manager even to survive on parson's pay with five kids. We knew he wouldn't have many dollars to leave us. But on that cool evening in Robert Lee, Texas, what he gave us and what we shared—love, respect, gratitude—can't be bought at any price. I think Dad felt pretty rich as we sat around that fire. I know I did.

Remember what Jesus said? "A man's life does not consist in the abundance of his possessions" (Luke 12:15).

Never has. Never will.

Now maybe you know what I mean when I say that the words you are reading are being written by a rich man.

And maybe you've already figured out that anybody who is rich in his father's love is wealthy.

And if Paul's prayer for you is becoming a reality and your eyes are being enlightened, maybe you also are seeing that regardless of what your earthly father is like, you and I share the very best Father of all. We're rich folks, you and I, already beginning to get a peek at the riches of the "glorious inheritance" that is ours because we're children of the Father.

How to Measure a Rainbow

Eyes Wide Open to God's Power

When Paul's prayer is answered and our eyes are enlightened, they'll be wide open to God's "incomparably great power for us who believe" (1:19).

Tomorrow morning, I'm taking a business trip. I'll drive to the airport. I'll answer security questions. I'll go through security gates, pick up a boarding pass, and line up with the rest of the herd to head down the chute where we'll be stuffed into the one-size-really-doesn't-fit-all seats of a Boeing 737. (They're really not all that bad unless you later need to get up or feel the need to breathe deeply.)

We'll settle in and listen, more or less, to the stewardess—excuse me, flight attendant—go through the safety spiel. Those of us who are sitting in the middle of the plane, near the emergency exits, will be asked if we'd be willing to open the emergency door if the plane gets in trouble, and we'll assure the dear lady that, should the plane get in trouble, we'll be delighted to ditch the door whether she asks or not. Then we'll sit back and a little airport answer to a tug boat (but it's really a shove-boat) will push us out. And then . . . Then we'll feel the thrust of the jet engines, that plane will come alive, rumble over to the runway, roar with power, and blast its way into the air.

I love the power and the thrust and the feeling of piercing the sky. I'm still amazed that hundreds of tons of metal can fly. And, perhaps most amazing of all, the power, the thrust, that propels these metal monsters through the air is, well, air! Air pushed through the turbines of a jet engine.

Air in motion, wind, can be a very powerful thing. I'll never forget the warmth and the force of the blast that would catch us in the face when in the days before jetways we stood behind a fence waving goodbye to loved ones, and the jet would turn, and the wind from its engines would wash over us! You couldn't really see it, but you surely could feel it. And you could see what it could do as the big jet rolled away and prepared to "inherit the air."

Jesus wasn't talking about Boeing 737's when he spoke to the goodhearted Pharisee Nicodemus. But he reminded Nicodemus about the power of the wind when he said, "The wind blows wherever it pleases. You hear its sound, but you cannot tell where it comes from or where it is going" (John 3:8). And he told the Pharisee that God's Holy Spirit is like the wind. You can't see the Spirit, but you can feel the Spirit's power, and you can see that power at work in the lives of people "born of the Spirit." God's power lifts them up, and they are able to soar.

So Paul tells the Ephesians, and he tells us, to open our eyes to the "incomparably great power" of the Spirit. We can't see God's Spirit, but we can see what the Spirit does. We can see his power displayed in a now-empty tomb as through the mighty working of God's Spirit Christ defeated death and, wonder of wonders, now makes that same power available in your life and in mine.

Without that power, folks, we're grounded. We're standing on life's runway flapping our arms and wondering why we're not flying anywhere. But with that power, we soar, as if on eagle's wings, as God himself provides the power for our journey through life and into the sky.

Let God open your eyes, Paul says, and marvel at the "incomparably great power" at work in the lives of those who believe.

The apostle wants us to catch a vision. He wants the eyes of our heart to be enlightened.

He's the schoolmaster hovering over his pupils urging them to open their eyes to the truths he's given his life to teach.

He's the master pianist who knows that his student has all the musical notes down pat, and now all that is lacking is what is already there, if he can just help the young one find it—the joy of the music. Ah, finding that joy is a far deeper thing than just getting all of the notes right.

And, yes, I admit it, he's the school nurse who knows better, far better than the stubborn little near-sighted nincompoop staring blindly at the eye chart, that the world really does look better in focus.

Paul knows that if our eyes are to be opened, it will have to be God who gets it done. We see so poorly on our own.

We're myopics who barely see.

We see things out of focus.

We focus on the wrong things.

We need someone praying for us that God will help us to see.

God is indeed the One who can help us see, and a very noteworthy example of that happening took place once upon a time a long time ago, a long time even before Paul's time. I love the delightful and intriguing story from 2 Kings 6.[8]

Way back in the 9th Century B.C., an Aramean king had a problem. At first, he was pretty sure it was a spy problem. He was at war with Israel. It wasn't anything approaching the magnitude of "world war," just a recurring border clash, but he and his were routinely winning. The Arameans were strong enough, and the Israelites weak enough, that he seems to have grown accustomed to having his way with them pretty regularly.

And then things went bad. From an Aramean point of view.

The Aramean king would confer with his officers, they would plan the next battle and decide where next to encamp, and (this is the amazing part!) Elisha the prophet, just as surely as if he'd bugged the war room, would go to the king of Israel and warn him, "Be careful about passing that place because that's where the Arameans are heading!"

The Israelite king learned to trust this priestly spy because time and again Elisha would warn the king who would send out scouts who would in turn discover that Elisha's information was always dead on target.

Pretty neat deal for the Israelites.

But the king of Aram was absolutely enraged and ready to draw blood. If he had to prime his blade by shedding Aramean blood before dipping his sword in Israelite blood, so be it. He had a spy in the camp, he was sure of it, and he demanded of his officers, "Which one of us is on the side of the king of Israel?"

You know the tone.

It's the tone parents use when they've had it with their offspring and the guilty party had better 'fess up or everyone is about to get spanked and, So what?, the parents reason, even you not-so-guilty pups have probably missed some paddlings you deserved anyway. They probably wouldn't really do it, you know, but the kids aren't so sure of that!

It's the tone the teacher uses when the class has pushed all of her buttons, and she finally announces to the whole class, "If one more of you says a word, every last one of you will be writing a five hundred word essay due tomorrow. Count on it!"

It's exactly the tone truly frustrated kings of old and modern despots of all sorts use when they want their advisors to realize that they're more than willing to trade in their old advisors for new ones—and the sort of mandatory retirement they have in mind won't cost the kingdom a cent.

The Aramean advisors recognized the tone.

"Will you not tell me which of us is on the side of the king of Israel?"

"None of us, my Lord the king," a sweaty-palmed officer

whined, and he quickly pointed the finger back toward Israel: "Elisha the prophet who is in Israel tells the king of Israel the very words you speak in your bedroom!"

"Find him!" ordered the king, "so I can deal with him once and for all," and find him they did. Word came back that Elisha was in Dothan, and the king immediately dispatched chariots (the ancient equivalent of modern tanks), horsemen, and troops to deal with the troublesome prophet.

And then the scene shifts.

Aramean chariots roll into Dothan in the middle of one dark night. If they break the silence, no one hears. Undetected, they surround the city.

Chariots.

Horsemen.

Troops.

As the morning sun begins to break over the horizon, Elisha's servant is doing whatever prophets' servants do in the early morning. He's still wiping the sleep out of his eyes when he stumbles outside, maybe to get the newspaper. He stoops down, grimaces when his stiff back reminds him that the ground is farther away than it once was, growls and mutters something about how when he was a boy paperboys had to land the thing on the porch, looks up, and as far as the eye can see, on all sides, stand Aramean chariots and horsemen.

Scared spitless, the servant rushes back to Elisha in an absolute panic.

"Oh, my master, what shall we do?"

"Don't be afraid!" the great prophet answers. "Those who are with us are more than those who are with them."

Then Elisha prays a prayer for his servant not so very different from Paul's prayer for the Ephesians and Paul's prayer for us: "O Lord, open his eyes so he may see."

And God opens the servant's eyes.

"Enlightened Eyes"

And he looks.

And he sees.

He sees—all around the hills surrounding the Arameans who had surrounded Elisha—God's army, horses and chariots of fire before whom the Arameans look very small indeed.

It's a wonderful story of God's power. (And you really should turn over to 2 Kings 6 and read the end of the story; it will surprise you!)

Where's the miracle? That God sent horses and chariots of fire to guard his servant Elisha? Yes, but just as much a tribute to the power of God is his hearing Elisha's prayer and opening the eyes of a very frightened servant to help him see what Elisha through faith-enlightened eyes had already seen—that those who are with us, if we're on God's side, are far greater than those who are with our foes.

Dear God, enlighten our eyes.

Chapter 3

As for you, you were dead in your transgressions and sins, in which you used to live when you followed the ways of this world and of the ruler of the kingdom of the air, the spirit who is now at work in those who are disobedient. All of us also lived among them at one time, gratifying the cravings of our sinful nature and following its desires and thoughts. Like the rest, we were by nature objects of wrath. But because of his great love for us, God, who is rich in mercy, made us alive with Christ even when we were dead in transgressions—it is by grace you have been saved. And God raised us up with Christ and seated us with him in the heavenly realms in Christ Jesus, in order that in the coming ages he might show the incomparable riches of his grace, expressed in his kindness to us in Christ Jesus. For it is by grace you have been saved, through faith—and this not from yourselves, it is the gift of God—not by works, so that no one can boast. For we are God's workmanship, created in Christ Jesus to do good works, which God prepared in advance for us to do.

Ephesians 2:1-10

The Post Office,
the Pharisees, and Lazarus

For it is by grace you have been saved, through faith—
and this not from yourselves, it is the gift of God—
not by works, so that no one can boast.
EPHESIANS 2:8-9

just witnessed a Post Office patron almost "go postal." The U. S. Postal Service must hate that phrase, but, I promise you, it well describes what I just saw. I'd innocently walked into the Post Office through the front door, past the box area, and on through the glass doors into the inner sanctum. I was hoping to return some packaged pants (a pants-too-small/preacher-too-fat sort of problem). What I got instead was an earful.

I decided pretty quickly that the better part of wisdom was to retreat somewhere out of range. Neither postmaster nor patron were in any mood to need or appreciate an audience. But, as I backed out of the door, I heard the patron intone with deep feeling, genuine frustration, and not just a little venom, "Why don't you just put a stamp on it?!" (If you want to get a feel for the tone, you can play those words to the tune of, "Why don't you just put a cork in it?!" "Why don't you take this job and . . . ?!" "Why don't you take a flying leap off . . . ?!" That sort of thing.)

This was not a "disgruntled postal employee" situation (though a few more mornings like this could certainly produce one), but that postal patron was most definitely disgruntled. He was about two seconds away from blowing a fuse or beating up a bureaucrat.

How to Measure a Rainbow

When the patron finally fumed out the door (he and I usually exchange "Good mornings" but I felt he'd probably like to be left alone, and I ducked behind a "thank you" note), I carefully ventured back into the inner sanctum only to hear one employee remark, "And then he said, 'What are you going to do? Put me in jail?'" Whatever postmaster and patron had exchanged, they had obviously gotten far afield from "Good morning."

Now, understand, the patron in question is not a bad guy. I've known him for years. Yes, he may at times be a little long of opinion and short of fuse, but he's long been an upstanding and contributing member of our community. (For what it's worth, he's been here a long time before that postmaster came, and he'll be here a long time after he's long gone.)[1]

What set him off? What caused this early morning fireworks display? What was the patron's problem?

I'm pretty sure I know. Although our relatively new postmaster is not at all a bad sort himself—in fact, he's a very likable, conscientious, and community-minded guy—he's the local head-honcho of a national bureaucracy, and he's got a few folks riled by a proliferation of regulations. His rules? The bureaucracy's rules? Who knows whose rules? That's part and parcel of the problem with bureaucracies.

But if this morning's postal patron had peppered the postmaster with buckshot, I know a couple of church secretaries, usually mild-mannered, sweet sorts, who would cheerfully help scald his USPS-certified hide, pluck his feathers, and throw him into a pot to create some sort of bureaucrat bullion base.

Gone are the days, you see, when Florence Smith's little niece over in Amarillo can address a note simply to "Aunt Flo, Muleshoe, Texas," drop it in the box, and be pretty confident a smiling postman will deliver the epistle to a smiling and thankful Aunt Flo.

The Post Office, the Pharisees, and Lazarus

Machines don't smile when they read addresses. That I can understand.

And postmasters may not smile as much as they once did, either. Not if they have many days like our postmaster had this morning. And they don't seem to hang around little towns as long as they did in days gone by. Consequently, they may not know Aunt Flo. That I can understand, too.

But what I don't understand is why at least 20 of about 200 flyers our church recently sent out got kicked back on technicalities. Okay, so we didn't put the box number on those (we didn't know the box number), and we used the street address instead. It had always worked before. Everybody in town from the mayor down to the most intelligent yard dogs knows where those businesses are! Trust me, in Muleshoe, Texas, this is not complicated. But the flyers got bumped back with *"NMR"* scrawled across the front. (That means "No Mail Receptacle." You learn that when you see it fifteen or twenty times in a row.)

Now, I suppose the reasoning might be, "We could deliver these, but we're gonna kick 'em back so you folks will go ahead and sharpen up your mailing list." That may be reasonable. (In the good old days, a friend at the Post Office would see that they got delivered, make a note of the ones with "bad" addresses, and give us a courtesy call.) There are some fine folks and some good friends down at our Post Office, and, to their credit, they've helped us out a lot in the past. So has our new postmaster. He really is not a bad guy.

But something's changed.

Somebody down there at the Post Office, or somebody up there in the big USPS bureaucracy in the sky, has gotten seriously hung up on rules & regulations, legalities & lists, jots & tittles & technicalities. Somebody deep in the bowels of the bureaucracy likes rules better than he likes delivering the mail. And it shows.

The practical result is that postal patrons across our nation now are the ones about to "go postal," all the while thanking the Lord for e-mail and United Parcel Service!

I don't like dealing with bureaucracies. I have a hard time understanding how they think. Or if they think. And who, by the way, is *they*?

If I buy a product at a local business, I almost always know the owner. I know him. He knows me. I can go to him with a problem, and he cares. He wants my business. It's to his advantage and to mine that I be a happy customer. He wants me to come back. He wants to be able to wave and smile when we pass each other on the street and for both of us to have a good feeling when I shake his hand tonight at the basketball game where we both have kids playing.

He owns his business. Maybe a problem will come up with his product or his service that he can't completely solve, but I know he'll try. It's *his* business. How it and his products perform reflects directly on him, and he knows it, and he cares. About his business. About his product. About me, his customer.

I'll try not to abuse the relationship. If his business closes each day at 5:00 p.m., I'll try not to come in at 4:58 with a thirty-minute-long problem. But if I had to do that, I'll betcha he'd stay. And if he's just heading out for lunch but notices that more customers have just come through the door than his available employees can easily handle, he'll stay put. He'll work through lunch if he needs to. It's his business. He owns it.

On the other hand, saying that we all own a government bureaucracy amounts to about the same thing as saying that nobody does. Who ultimately is responsible for how it runs? Can you find his or her name? What are the chances you'll get to have a good conversation with him? Ever notice how in most bureaucratic offices, nobody cares how many folks are in line? Or how long you have to wait? Or whether or not there's a long line when it's break time and "I'm outa here!"? Most of their employees don't really care what the forms say or how long it took you to fill them out. They just want the bureaucratic "i's" dotted and the "t's" crossed. And they want it in triplicate. They don't care if they (because it's not really *them*, you see) owe you or you owe them. They care very little if the amount is $1 or $10,000. They just want it listed in the right blank on the right form in the right color of ink.

It's not their money.

It's not their business.

It's no skin off their nose, one way or the other.

It's a bureaucracy, not a business.

Such a business would go bankrupt. Quickly. But not such a bureaucracy. It's not personal. It's mechanical. Because machines can't care, it doesn't care about the people, patrons and employees alike, who get ground up in its gears, frustrated by its endless forms, and regularly robbed by its ridiculous regulations.

Hmm. It occurs to me that I may have jumped up on a soapbox here! Maybe allowed myself a little tirade. Stroked a pet peeve. Pounded the pulpit. Sorry. But I'll bet you agree.

I don't like dealing with bloodless bureaucracies.

When Religion Becomes Bureaucratic

I like it even less when religion becomes bureaucratic and faith becomes bloodless and cross-less, the kind of do-it-yourself hair-splitting self-worship that tries to pass for piety.

It can happen, you know.

Some people seem to be more concerned with rituals, regulations, and rules than with relationship. They see God as more of a cold bureaucrat than a warm and loving Father. They could practice their religion and peddle their faith every bit as well if Christ had never come and the cross had never happened. The focus of their faith is them, not Him. They know very little about pardon. They know nothing about power. (After all, without the cross there is no pardon and no tomb, and without the empty tomb, there is no resurrection power.) They end up being very unhappy people. And they end up wanting you to be, too.

Maybe it's not a conscious thing with them, but they act the way they do, they relate to God the way they do, because they really halfway expect to get to Heaven and meet a bureaucrat at the gate. Some heavenly (more hellish, really) pencil-pushing, code-quoting, tome-toting gatekeeper intoning to the poor guy just ahead of them in line, "Well, sir, we'd really like to let you in, but according to our records you failed to file **Form 5501-5b, revised** back on February 1, 1946, and there's just no way now. Not possible. No, we're mightily sorry, but rules are rules, you know, and if we make an exception in your case, why, all sorts of people will be wanting to get in here completely on the basis of mercy and grace. And, of course, we just can't have that. Next."

When he walked the roads of Palestine, Jesus ran into—or had run-ins with—more than a few folks of just this variety.

Maybe you have, too.

The Scribes and Pharisees

Years ago, I sat in on a meeting of the scribes and Pharisees. Oh, no one called it that, but I assure you, that's what it was. I met with this group of preachers and church leaders once a month or so to eat a sandwich and discuss Scripture. On this particular occasion, I was the host pastor. First time. Last time.

We sat in the fellowship hall of the church I was then serving. People and their lives came into the conversation occasionally and were briefly considered. But it became apparent that the religious leaders convened that day were much more interested in rules than they were in people. They were a lot more inclined to administer law than they were to minister to people.

The Post Office, the Pharisees, and Lazarus

I should mention that in many ways these were very good folks. Which is one thing that makes the whole scene so frightening.

These were people who had dedicated their lives to ministry. Most were preachers. All were church leaders. One or two or a few had been missionaries. They were committed people. People who had worked hard and sacrificed to do what they considered to be the most important work on earth. As to works of law, as to zeal, as to commitment, I assure you, they were blameless.

But they were bureaucrats. Religious bureaucrats.

We were drinking coffee. Visiting. Talking about Scripture. Were we talking about Paul's words regarding elders and deacons in 1 Timothy? Were we discussing Christ's words in the Sermon on the Mount regarding divorce (Matthew 5)? I don't recall. But somehow both subjects became the focus of the conversation, and somebody shared a story.

I am quite sure I have changed some of the details that follow. Not to protect the innocent—or the guilty, for that matter—but because this all happened a long time ago and I'm fuzzy now about some small details. It seems, though, that a church the storyteller had once served in some capacity was just about to honor a fine old gentleman and his wife who were celebrating their Golden Wedding Anniversary.

Fifty years of marriage.

Fifty years together.

For decades of those years, this well-respected gentleman had served that church as an elder. A rich heritage. A rich history. Now it was time to bestow richly-deserved honor on a good man and the loving and lovely wife who had served by his side.

But just a day or two before the celebration, the old gentleman stumbled into the office of his preacher. Something was obviously wrong. The minister could not imagine what the problem could be, but the old man broke down in tears and through his sobs "confessed" that the woman to whom he had been married for fifty years was not his first wife. More than half a century ago, as an impetuous teenager about to go off to war, he'd married another woman. The marriage had lasted barely as long as the ink on the hastily-procured marriage license and not nearly as long as the war. But married he had been. Very briefly. And hardly anyone knew.

Now he was unburdening his soul from the weight of what he considered to be a terrible secret, a hidden failure he felt so acutely that had he been an axe murderer confessing his despicable decades-old secret to a judge, he could hardly have been more terribly crushed by the weight of his sin or more deeply wounded by poignant grief and gut-wrenching guilt.

What should he do? You see, given his group's understanding of Scripture, he had not really had the "right" to remarry. And, by the same (mistaken, I think) token, he was not "qualified" to be an elder. He'd led a good life, built a fine marriage and home with godly children (who knew nothing about that early marriage), and served the church unselfishly. But he was afraid that much of his life had been based on a lie and that all of the good he had done had been annulled by a mistake he'd made years ago.

What, oh, what, should he do? In utter anguish, he asked the man of God before him.

And what would this man say?

What solace would he offer?

What counsel would he give?

I wondered, but it seems the counselor in question had little doubt.

"You must publicly confess your sin," he advised. And he went on to tell the man that, if he was to have any hope at all of eternal salvation, he must divorce his wife of fifty years, find his former wife, and marry her (at great inconvenience to her since this course of action would most likely require another divorce on her part as well). Or he must remain alone. And, of course, his continuing to serve the church in any leadership capacity was completely out of the question.

I honestly don't remember what action the old man actually took. As I recall, and I fervently hope I am mistaken, the story-teller said that the old man did indeed leave his wife. Whether he found the first lady or lived alone for his remaining years, I have no idea.

This story was told a long time ago. And I should have listened more closely. But my head was spinning at the realization that, first, a religious lawyer would claim to speak for God as he counseled a man to leave his wife of fifty years, and, second, that a group of assembled church leaders would assent that, yes, indeed, that was exactly the correct counsel. I was amazed and ashamed that they would react to such a thing with arrogant affirmation and not with tears.

Can you for a moment imagine our Lord giving such counsel?

Oh, the scribes and the Pharisees of 2,000 years ago could not possibly have out-done the scribes and Pharisees re-convened in that fellowship hall in Texas less than twenty years ago. No religious bureaucrat of any time could have done a better job of ignoring the screams and the pain of those caught in the gears of his bureaucratic machine.

Riddled by his regulations.

Condemned by his code.

Crushed by the weight of his law.

Kindred Spirits

Consider the story in Luke 13, and tell me if you see any difference at all in the scribes and Pharisees of Jesus' day and the scribes and Pharisees of our own:

How to Measure a Rainbow

On a Sabbath Jesus was teaching in one of the synagogues, and a woman was there who had been crippled by a spirit for eighteen years. She was bent over and could not straighten up at all. When Jesus saw her, he called her forward and said to her, "Woman, you are set free from your infirmity." Then he put his hands on her, and immediately she straightened up and praised God.

Indignant because Jesus had healed on the Sabbath, the synagogue ruler said to the people, "There are six days for work. So come and be healed on those days, not on the Sabbath."

The Lord answered him, "You hypocrites! Doesn't each of you on the Sabbath untie his ox or donkey from the stall and lead it out to give it water? Then should not this woman, a daughter of Abraham, whom Satan has kept bound for eighteen long years, be set free on the Sabbath day from what bound her?"

When he said this, all his opponents were humiliated, but the people were delighted with all the wonderful things he was doing.

(Luke 13:10-20)

Jesus sees the person and the pain, and he heals. The Pharisees see only the broken law, and they condemn.

The once-crippled woman receives healing, and she praises God. The Pharisees see the healing, and they complain about a code violation.

Jesus sees a daughter of Abraham and a child of the King who should not be bound by Satan, and he releases her from her bondage. But the assembled religious bureaucrats care more about their oxen than they do about a child of God.

After all, nobody filled out the right form. This healing was not up to code.

Not legal.

Not lawful.

Not allowed.

"No healings without a permit." And you can't get one of

those on the Sabbath, so the verdict on this healing is obvious.

Not permitted.

The scribes and Pharisees, then and now, are the ones who "load people down with rules and regulations, nearly breaking their backs, but never lift even a finger" to help them carry those burdens.[2] After all, as far as the modern-day bunch I lunched with were concerned, the lady being bereft of her husband wasn't their wife of fifty years. Their children and grandchildren weren't part of this family in anguish. Their lives were not the lives being ripped apart by this Pharisaic counsel.

Like their counterparts of old, if they could reach down and pick up a stone, they would grasp it quickly because their religion is all about stone. Tables of stone.

They know a lot about law and nothing about the warm heart of God.

They know more about code violations than about the cross of Christ.

They focus much more on sin than on the Savior.

Even the Pharisees of old, remember, were wise enough to drop the stones they were holding when Jesus turned their gaze from the adulterous woman sprawled in the dirt before him to the sin of their own lives.[3] But not these, their modern-day counterparts.

Pharisees are Pharisees whether they're found in first-century Palestine or in a fellowship hall in Texas.

Here's what you must do, they say, to atone for your own sin and earn forgiveness. They forget that only one Person's sacrifice is powerful enough to ever really cover our sin and that what he would give can only be received as a gift. But they can't tell us about what they have never experienced. If they would just un-clinch their fists and drop their stones, then they could open their hands to receive as a gift the pardon of God's Son and the power of God's Spirit that makes it possible for us to become what God has called us to be.

Pharisees, then and now, are the ones who would "travel over land and sea" to win one convert and, when they do, make him twice as much a child of hell as themselves.[4]

For Pharisees, then and now, the focus of religion is on what you must do. For Christ, the focus of faith is on what God has done and will do for his people.

Pharisees, then and now, know all about ritual and regulation and rules but nothing about relationship. Here's what you must know, they say. But God says, Here is *who* you must know. My Son.

No wonder the Pharisees were shamed by Christ.

No wonder the people were delighted by him.

The Business of God

The business of God is proper religion and pious ritual, said the Pharisees. No, said Jesus, the business of God is redeeming people and lifting them up by his love.

The business of the Post Office is not to fill out forms; it is to deliver letters. If the forms help get the letters delivered, help get that primary job done, well and good, but . . .

The business of God's people is to know God through his Son and to be made like him, and how do you get that done?

You don't. He does.

All of our ritual, all of God's laws, every precept and command, is designed to help us place ourselves in positions of trust so God can get the job done and do the work that needs to be done in our lives as he molds us into the image of his Son.

God's job is to work; our job is to trust. And don't kid yourself. Trusting is a full-time job.[5]

The Post Office, the Pharisees, and Lazarus

You really ought to try to address your letters correctly. It's easier on everybody that way.

But what happens when you don't?

Then you're at the mercy of a postmaster, a mail carrier, or a postal service machine.

We really ought to always follow all of God's commands and keep his will perfectly.

But, no big surprise here, often we don't. What then?

Then we have to make a choice between the only two ways of salvation ever offered.

Grace or works.

Mercy or merit.

A code or a cross.

Then we have to read Ephesians 2 as it would be written by a Pharisee or as it really was written by Paul.

A Pharisee would point his finger at your very obvious faults: "Your only dim hope of salvation is by law, through works—for God gives us nothing we don't earn. God only 'helps those who help themselves.'[6] The Bible says you were created "to do good works" (notice how Pharisees use just enough Scripture to sound scriptural, and they never give you the whole story), and perhaps you can do enough of them to be saved by the skin of your teeth.[7] So get to work, worm! Work, sweat, and tremble. And while you're at it, pray that Christ doesn't return or you don't drop dead before you've worked enough. And how will you ever know you've worked enough? Oh, you won't, but just keep working, sweating, trembling, living in utter dejection and fear."[8]

That's how a Pharisee would put it.

But what Paul actually says is that God, completely aware

that we were once dead in our transgressions, has in his rich mercy raised us up in Christ, even when we were dead, to show us "the incomparable riches of his grace," for "it is by grace you have been saved, through faith—and this not from yourselves, it is the gift of God—not by works, so that no one can boast" (2:4-9).

That's good news! That's the Gospel!

And as for works, the real work is God's. And the entire universe marvels in amazement at the workmanship of the God who works in the lives of his children.

His is the power that saves us.

His is the power that makes us holy.

His is the power at work within us enabling us to do the good works "God prepared in advance for us to do" (2:10).

Not *for* salvation.

Because of it.

We began this chapter with the Post Office. I want to end it with Lazarus.

You don't see the connection? Have you never heard of dead letters? Sorry.

Old Lazarus was dead. Dead as a doornail. You need to understand that, or, as Charles Dickens once wrote about the similarly dead Jacob Marley, "nothing wonderful can come of the story I am going to relate."[9]

Lazarus, Jesus' dear friend from Bethany, near Jerusalem, was dead. He'd fallen ill sometime after Jesus had been chased across the Jordan River and into the region of Perea by his enemies. There Jesus gets word that Lazarus is gravely ill, but the Lord announces, "This sickness will not end in death. No, it is for God's glory so that God's Son may be glorified through it" (John 11:4).[10]

But Jesus had waited two more days before heading back to Bethany.

"Lazarus has fallen asleep," he explained to his disciples who by this time are probably wondering if Christ has forgotten about Lazarus and almost hoping that he has.

"Let's go wake him up."

The disciples are a little hesitant. They remind Jesus, as if he needed reminding, that they had just been chased out of Judea and that men over there across the Jordan, men with swords, would like nothing better than for them to return.

"If Lazarus is sleeping, he'll wake up just fine on his own," they reason. And it will be a lot healthier for us if we have nothing to do with the wakeup call.

Then Jesus says plainly, "Lazarus is dead, and for your sake I am glad I was not there, so you may believe. But let us go to him."

We do well to recall that it was Thomas, the one later dubbed "The Doubter," the disciple turned by temperament to be pessimistic, but who would rather die than be disloyal to his Lord, who said, "Let us also go, that we may die with him."

And they go.

When they reach Bethany, they find that Lazarus has already been in the tomb for four days, and his sisters, Mary and Martha, are themselves entombed in grief.

Martha seems to hold out some tenuous hope. One moment she seems to hold hope for present resurrection; another moment, just for something "in the last day," by and by. She doesn't know what to think, what to hope.

Mary just says, as Martha already has, "Lord, if you'd just been here, my brother wouldn't have died."

Too late now, though.

But maybe at least you can go out to the cemetery and pay your respects, take a look at the family plot, lay a carnation out in front of the stone, and just wish that something could have been done sooner.

In time, you know. Before it was too late, and Lazarus had died, and the body had been buried, and the funeral director had cashed the check.

Jesus is deeply moved. He asks where they have laid him, and he weeps.

Out at the cemetery, Jesus tells them to take away the stone which covers the entrance to the tomb. Martha, always the practical one, warns, "Lord, he's been dead for four days. There will be a terrible odor."

But Jesus simply says, "Did I not tell you that if you believed, you would see the glory of God?"

They roll away the stone.

Jesus prays to the Father.

And in a loud voice, loud enough to wake the dead as God's power surges through the tomb to rob the grave, he commands, "Lazarus, come forth!"

And Lazarus does!

He's covered in the trappings of the grave. Strips of linen. A cloth around his face. But at Jesus' bidding, the amazed mourners whose hearts almost stopped the moment Lazarus' was restarted release the resurrected Lazarus from the grave clothes. No grave clothes needed here. Lazarus is alive!

Many people who saw what Jesus did believe. But the chief priests and the Pharisees resolve to fill another tomb. Jesus, they reasoned, was becoming too great a threat. Jesus, they reasoned, must die.

The Post Office, the Pharisees, and Lazarus

We're Like Lazarus

Did you realize how much you and I have in common with old Lazarus?

Like him, we were dead. Dead in sin, and helpless as dead people to do anything about it.

We're tempted to think that maybe God could have done something. If he'd just gotten here sooner, you know. If he had come on the scene before we really fouled up.

But now the die has been cast, and we're dead.

The deed has been done.

The divorce has been decreed.

The devilment has been undertaken.

The down and dirty deal with Satan has been struck.

Depression.

Despair.

Despondence.

Disrepute.

Disgust.

Down we've tumbled. And we're dead.

And it's too late now.

We've been dead so long, there is such a terrible stench. Nothing to be done now. Right?

Wrong.

Jesus sees.

Jesus weeps.

Jesus wraps our sin around himself, hangs on a cross, and dies.

Jesus puts on grave clothes laid out for us.

Jesus lies in a tomb meant for us, but not for long.

Jesus bursts forth with new life he means to share. With us. For all time.

But we're dead, right?

Wrong.

We were. Just as dead as Lazarus. Dead as doornails and

with just as little capacity to grant ourselves life by any power of our own.

But it was when we were dead that God reached down to raise us up.

God split open the tomb.

God gave us life. His life.

God unwrapped the grave clothes.

God seated us at the table with his Son.

And it's the strangest thing. Back before we died, we never drank so deeply of his joy! But now we're really alive.

And what did we do to deserve that life? Nothing! Don't you see? Dead doornails don't do much.

We were dead, but now we're alive, and now we know the right question. What did God do?

Everything.

By grace.

Through faith.

In the gift of his Son.

Once we were dead as a doornail. But now we're alive. And if you understand that, something wonderful indeed can come of this tale.

Chapter 4

Therefore, remember that formerly you who are Gentiles by birth and called "uncircumcised" by those who call themselves "the circumcision" (that done in the body by the hands of men)—remember that at that time you were separate from Christ, excluded from citizenship in Israel and foreigners to the covenants of the promise, without hope and without God in the world. But now in Christ Jesus you who once were far away have been brought near through the blood of Christ.

For he himself is our peace, who has made the two one and has destroyed the barrier, the dividing wall of hostility, by abolishing in his flesh the law with its commandments and regulations. His purpose was to create in himself one new man out of the two, thus making peace, and in this one body to reconcile both of them to God through the cross, by which he put to death their hostility. He came and preached peace to you who were far away and peace to those who were near. For through him we both have access to the Father by one Spirit.

Consequently, you are no longer foreigners and aliens, but fellow citizens with God's people and members of God's household, built on the foundation of the apostles and prophets, with Christ Jesus himself as the chief cornerstone. In him the whole building is joined together and rises to become a holy temple in the Lord. And in him you too are being built together to become a dwelling in which God lives by his Spirit.

Ephesians 2:11-22

A Hole in the Wall

For he himself is our peace, . . .
and has destroyed the barrier,
the dividing wall of hostility, . . .
EPHESIANS 2:14

W hat I really needed this week was a hole in the wall. In my study. A hole. No kidding! I really did. And I was able to drill and saw and punch a pretty good hole through some paneling and sheetrock, past the studs and the board used for a moisture barrier.

But then I hit the brick. And I gained new respect for would-be jail breakers who use little pilfered bits of steel to spend months trying to saw through mortar and bars. I was equipped with a drill, a hammer, and chisels, and I still had a tough time.

Part of the problem had to do with the execution of the plan. I drilled for fifteen minutes just trying to get one little pilot hole through some very ordinary-looking mortar. And it didn't take nearly that long pounding away with a hammer and chisel for me to realize that my chisel just wasn't up to the task. Execution was a problem.

But another part of the problem not to be overlooked was the plan itself. I really didn't just need a hole in the wall; I needed a hole in the wall in the right spot.

Getting a hole in the wall, period, wouldn't be easy. Getting a hole in the wall in the right spot so that the new air conditioner I was installing would stick in and stick out in all the right places might take a minor miracle.

How to Measure a Rainbow

I thought of those engineers planning that magnificent stainless steel arch on the banks of the Mississippi in St. Louis, the Gateway to the West. The intricate planning required to start that huge monument on both ends at the bottom and finally get it to meet perfectly at the top boggled my mind. I was trying to get two holes to line up across a ten-inch space, and I, for one, wouldn't have placed a bet on my own success!

So I called for help. I called for Joe Harbin, one of our church's elders who is a woodworking wizard, to come and add his considerable carpentry skills to my meagre ones—and to be there for a second opinion on my measurements. And I called for bricklayer Ronnie Garcia to come and cut out the appropriate brick, which he did in less time than it took me to eat lunch. With the help of fellows who knew what they were doing, the hole in the outside of the wall matched perfectly with the hole on the inside of the wall, and the office is now deliciously cool.

I learned something last week. I learned that it's not all that easy to punch the right kind of hole in a wall. I learned that, if you plan to try, you'd better get the right kind of help.

Once a wall is up, it doesn't usually come down very easily. But if there is one thing we humans are good at, it's building walls.

The Walls We Build

For almost fifty years, the wall separating East from West, Communism from democracy, enslavement from freedom, divided the city of Berlin and stood as a solid and stark reminder that the wall between East and West in this world was far thicker than even the formidable one we could see fashioned out of brick and mortar and concertina wire.

But the Berlin wall came down. And, as the world has continued to watch in amazed gratitude, the wall between East and West dividing much of this world has, in many ways, continued to come down with it. Not as easily or quickly as we might like. But that it's come down at all is a wonderful blessing! And we've been privileged to see democracy and freedom take root in places and in ways that most of us never in our wildest dreams thought we'd live to see.

It's an amazing and hopeful thing to see a wall of hatred and distrust come down. It happens altogether too rarely.

Lots of walls litter the landscape of Planet Earth.

Ever since the time of old Abraham, when his sons fussed, and Ishmael went one way and Isaac went the other, when half-brothers chose to focus on the half that divided rather than the half that they shared in common, the Holy Land has been the setting for some very unholy hatred.

A reporter once asked Israeli prime minister Golda Meir when the Arabs and Israelis would ever quit fighting. Mrs. Meir replied, "When the Arabs love their children more than they hate us."[1] But you and I know that the deep hatred behind that ponderous wall goes both ways. It always does. And, as long as one side waits for the other to make the first move toward real peace, those walls only grow taller and harder to scale.

The mortar that keeps the walls up is hatred. And you can be sure that the inmates imprisoned on both sides of a wall will do their part to chink the cracks in the mortar joints with more of the hateful stuff as soon as there appears to be any hope that a wall might show signs of coming down.

Our world has a morbid fascination with walls. The walls imprison us, but they also make us feel comfortable. We too easily forget that a prison with which we're familiar is still a prison.

But we're frightened to let the walls come down because we might see other folks who look a lot like us. People who are sometimes perplexed. Sometimes hurt. Sometimes unsure of their direction. Sometimes right, but often wrong and in need of forgiveness.

Just like us.

Who knows? If we looked at them long enough, if we really looked at them with unjaundiced eyes and, before we opened our mouths to speak in hatred, we opened our ears to hear and understand their very real pain, we might forget that the folks on the other side of the walls we build are supposed to be our enemies!

But, much more often than not, our ears stay closed, and the walls stay up. In Northern Ireland they divide Catholic and Protestant. In the Balkans they divide Croat and Serb. In Los Angeles, they divide Black and White.

In families they divide husband and wife, mother and daughter, father and son.

In the church, they divide Baptist and Church of Christ, Methodist and Lutheran, Pentecostal and Presbyterian.

And on and on we divide and are conquered.

Walls of Religious Division

Sad to say, nowhere will we find a more despoiled and wall-littered landscape than in the realm of religion.

Once walled off, Baptists keep on building walls to further divide Southern Baptists from Missionary Baptists, Free Will Baptists from Primitive Baptists, etc. Some years ago Baptists began marking off territory for a new wall between moderates and conservatives. And my good Baptist colleagues in ministry are candid enough to frankly say what most folks suspected anyway, that the struggle is more over power than theology. Church splits almost always are, and that's every bit as true no matter what the brand name is on the label. The Baptists have no corner on division.

A Hole in the Wall

Lutherans put up walls between Evangelical Lutheran Church of America Lutherans and Missouri Synod Lutherans. The Missouri Synod folks fire shots at the ELCA for accepting too many folks regardless of theology and watering down the faith and, so as to not make the same mistake, they themselves hardly do anything with anybody. The ELCA counters that Christ loved people with problems and maybe a little more mercy to a few more folks might not be a bad thing, but some of their own folks will tell you that they wonder if their group has forgotten that Christ also had some things to say about holiness and that loving the sinner is different from being complacently acquiescent in the face of sin.

Please don't misunderstand my words. I don't at all mean to pick on Baptists and Lutherans. They are in no way unique in this wall-building regard. Folks in my own religious tradition make exactly the same mistakes every bit as often.

In my own tradition, we have built more than a few walls of our own that we have had a hard time seeing around. And, like everyone else who is religious, I think we have to admit that at times in our history those walls have become more important to us than the Lord who is supposed to be the focal point of our faith.

What makes my own group's divided, walled-off situation even sadder is that this movement began with a stirring clarion call to unity. Unity in Christ was the passion of my tradition's founding fathers. This was a unity movement—that lasted less than 150 years before it had divided itself into three. And "my" third alone, the Church of Christ, has walled itself up behind, depending upon your method of computation, from six to well over twenty different brands, flavors, and sects.[2] And that, my friends, is to me a matter worthy of some sincere tears.

Storyteller Garrison Keillor tells of how his own religious forbearers, a group he calls the Sanctified Brethren, who look awfully similar to some of my own supposedly sanctified brethren, put up walls of their own.[3] Maybe we can learn something, by the way, by noticing how foolish and comical "religious issues" like these always look to everyone except those who own those particular issues. Religious combatants who are so involved in holy wars that they've put their common sense on hold always look silly to everybody except their fellow combatants!

One of the burning "issues" being dealt with by the Sanctified Brethren had to do with whether or not it was right to show hospitality to someone who was, as they put it, involved in religious error. (Offhand, can you think of anybody who is not? Can you name for me someone who is absolutely correct on every jot and tittle of the faith? And can you point me to someone who is not in serious trouble if our salvation is really based on being "right" on every issue instead of being based on being "right" about Jesus Christ?) Two factions of the Sanctified but split apart Brethren, opposing armies lined up behind a Brother Miller and a Brother Johnson, needed a demilitarized zone where they could meet without treading on each other's turf, and so, Keillor says, they were finally invited to meet at his Uncle Al's home. Uncle Al, who had family on both sides of the dispute, was grieved by the whole issue and was willing to try to "make peace between those two marbleheads and prevent a great deal of unhappiness for the rest" of the clan.[4]

Arranging for the meeting took weeks, but a Brother Fields who "had never shown hospitality to anyone, whether in error or not" and was therefore considered "neutral on the question" got everything arranged. The Millerites and Johnsonites showed up at Uncle Al's house, were invited in, sat "in awesome silence" in the living room until the call for dinner came, and then assembled around the dining room table "extended with two leaves so they wouldn't have to sit close."[5]

They bowed their heads for the prayer before the meal, but as Keillor writes,

A Hole in the Wall

Prayer was a delicate matter. Brethren were known to use even prayer before a meal as a platform, and so Al the peacemaker, concerned lest one brother take prayer and beat the others over the head with it, said, "Let us bow our heads in silent prayer, giving thanks for the meal," and they bowed their heads and closed their eyes and—a long time passed; . . . and soon it was clear that neither side wanted to stop before the other: they were seeing who could pray the longest.

Brother Miller peeked through his fingers at Brother Johnson, who was earnestly engaged in silent communion with the Lord, who agreed with him on so many things. His forehead almost touched the plate. So Brother Miller dove back into prayer and the other Brethren stayed under too, sneaking glances around the table to see if anyone else noticed how *long* it was. Minutes drifted by. Heads stayed bowed, nobody would come up. To stop praying might imply a weakness of faith.

Al said "Amen," to offer them a way out of the deadlock, and said it again: "*Amen.*" Brother Miller looked up and saw Johnson still bowed, so he went back down just as Johnson put his periscope up and saw Brother Miller submerged, so down *he* went. It was becoming the longest table grace in history, it ground on and on, and then Aunt Flo slid her chair back, rose, went to the kitchen, and brought out the food that they were competing to see who could be more thankful for. She set the hay down where the goats could get it. Tears ran down Brother Johnson's face. His eyes were clamped shut, and tears streamed down, and so was Brother Miller weeping.

It's true what they say, that smell is the key that unlocks our deepest memories, and with their eyes closed, the smell of fried chicken and gravy made those men into boys again. It was years ago, they were fighting, and a mother's voice from on high said, "You two stop it and get in here and have your dinners. Now. I mean it." The blessed cornmeal crust and rapturous gravy brought the memory to mind, and the stony hearts of the two giants melted; they raised their heads and filled their plates and slowly peace was made over that glorious chicken.[6]

81

How to Measure a Rainbow

We laugh, but only until we realize that we have more in common with the hardheads gathered at Uncle Al's and Aunt Flo's than we'd like to think. We've put up our own walls over the same sorts of non-issue issues. Ah, and how badly we all need an Aunt Flo and some sort of healing balm even if it comes in the form of the sweet-smelling grease of fried chicken!

In Heaven's Name

How in heaven's name do people split churches over how to care for orphans, or how many cups to use in communion, or whether or not a church can have a fellowship hall, or if it's okay to sing with a piano, or how to teach kids Bible stories? (I'm sure these issues will seem silly to you unless they happen to be *your* issues, but I'll wager you can name some teapot tempests from your own group that seem just as silly and petty to folks outside your group.) How in heaven's name do we justify fracturing the Body of Christ over such issues?

In Heaven's name, that's how.

In Heaven's name, we managed to find ways. In Heaven's name, my own tradition which began with a noble and stirring call to unity managed to put up walls to cut itself off from the larger Body of Christ as it became more and more fractured and isolated, exclusive and judgmental.

We cut ourselves off from other believers and, inside our own ranks, we littered the landscape with a score of new walls.

I don't mean to downgrade my own heritage, nor would I encourage you to disrespect yours. Much like yours, I imagine, my religious heritage did indeed have noble roots, and there is much about this little segment of Christendom which is still worthy of love and respect. It was here that I met Christ, and I thank God and dear Christians from within this tradition for the nurture and love which has been such a rich blessing in my life. And seeing many of "our" churches returning to what I think is best in our heritage, refusing to continue to fracture Christ's Body over "issues," and preaching simply "Christ and him crucified" (1 Corinthians 2:2) is a source of joy for me. There is a lot in my heritage to love (and many people who I love deeply who have graciously and richly loved me). I'm not sure that my religious tradition has been more divided and divisive than many others, but that's precious little comfort because I'm quite sure we've been no better. We've spent far too much time reinforcing walls that should never have been built.

Christians of all stripes, believers who should know better, from the first century on down to the present, have used religious-sounding labels to divide families and communities and split churches. And the Body of Christ bleeds.

Walls of hostility should never be welcomed, but in the church, of all places, they seem even more ghastly and garish and out of place.

We let walls divide us. With enmity and ignorance as bricks, we build walls around our traditions and our pet religious peeves and shut out others who refuse to share them or are walled in behind their own. It's hard to see around a wall, and we seem to take masochistic delight in building them nowhere higher than in the church.

Maybe that's why it can be so hard to see that on the other sides of the walls are folks who love the Lord just as much as we do. And who need his grace and forgiveness just as badly as we do.

We talk about how terrible it is that the Body is divided, and then someone with the kind of arrogance that can only be fueled by the fires of hell allows as how those folks wouldn't have to be separate from us if they'd just straighten up and see things our way. Like God does, you know.

And with thousands of others who make the same mistake we betray the fact that we really don't want the walls to come down. We just want more folks lined up with us behind the one that obscures our view.

Needed: A Wall Removal Expert

Walls. We're so good at building them. What we need is an expert to help us get them down! We need an expert in wall removal, and I'm convinced that there really is only one. Only One.

Only one brick Expert can tear down the walls we build. Ironic, isn't it? The only One who can knock down the walls we've built with stones of hatred is himself called the Cornerstone.

He's the Cornerstone of the temple of God. He's the foundation stone upon which God himself builds and anything worth building in this world is established. And he's the only One really qualified to tear down the walls of hatred that divide us.

In nations. In communities. In families. In the church. Only Jesus Christ himself can really tear down the walls.

When the God of the universe wrapped himself in humanity and put on human skin, he came into a world just as horribly divided then as it is now.

Arabs and Jews squabbled. Gentiles and Jews never in their wildest dreams (they probably would have called them nightmares) had any idea of singleness of heart and purpose one with the other. Oh, yes, the Romans were trying to unite the world, but for their own purposes. And they were doing it with a heavy hand and a sword.

On a more day-to-day, mundane level, I'm pretty sure that unity was no more a reality then in people's everyday life experience than it is now. I imagine that it was a stretch even then for lots of parents to understand lots of teenagers. Women probably fussed some to other women about the idiosyncrasies of men, and I have no doubt that even then men rolled their eyes, shook their heads, and wondered if they could ever comprehend how the possessors of two X chromosomes could be so much harder to understand than their brethren of the XY persuasion.

The walls were up! Between competing nations, religions, ethnic groups, and sexes. Just as they are today.

A Ponderous Wall

You may recall that by far the biggest barrier facing the young Christian church in its infancy was not persecution from without. No indeed. It was a question of "wall removal" that came from within!

A wall was up. The church didn't erect it, but she fell heir to it. The wall was up between Gentile and Jew. As far as anyone could remember, it always had been. And folks on both sides of the barrier could think of a thousand good reasons why that wall would always stand inviolate—and why it should.

It wasn't just that the Gentiles in town felt that the Jewish folks down at the clothiers had gouged their prices. No, those Jews were strange—deep down to the bone, strange. In a world where gods were a dime a dozen, those folks worshiped just one. And they were arrogant about it. Absolutely intolerant. Wherever the phrase, "live and let live" came from, it wasn't from the Jewish Quarter. As far as the Gentiles were concerned, those Jews did everything they could to make it hard to be civil to them. So fine. The Gentiles wouldn't try. You Jews want the wall up? It's okay with us.

And things were no better on the other side. Down at First Jewish Church, Jerusalem, the elders could and did quote plenty of Scripture to try to prove that God shared their opinion that Jews should have nothing to do with Gentiles. After all, those filthy folks worshiped idols. They were pagan heathens. These sentiments weren't exactly from Scripture, but they were almost Scripture in the minds of the Jews: Gentiles are sorrier than dirt! God created Gentiles to be fuel for the fires of hell!

The wall was up in a big way. And the church inherited the wall.

This won't be news to you, but don't forget that the apostles were all Jewish. They're still reeling from the events of the crucifixion and resurrection. It's been a real tussle for them to begin to learn that Jesus would be far more than just a Jewish national King, and now the Holy Spirit is beginning to teach them that Jesus is much more than just a Jewish Savior.

The Spirit had to hit Peter on the head with a rock from Heaven with a note attached to the effect that Gentiles also had a place in the young Christian church. It took a lot to get Peter's attention as the Spirit led him up to his roof and the sheet came down from Heaven full of unclean animals, and Peter, the Jew who'd never touched an unclean animal, was told to kill and eat.

You think doctors don't make house calls? Neither did Jews if the house in question belonged to a Gentile. But before long God had Peter, the Jew, ringing the bell at the home of Cornelius, the Gentile, welcoming him into the Christian church![7]

It took a vision from God to get Peter to do it.

It took a blinding light from Heaven and a vision of Christ himself to get the Jewish prodigy Saul of Tarsus to change course, stop persecuting Christians, and, of all things, become the apostle to the Gentiles, Paul.[8] (I love commentator F. F. Bruce's description of Paul as "the apostle of the heart set free," and indeed that's what he became![9])

It took a big church business meeting in Jerusalem and the

strong leading of the Holy Spirit himself (you can read about it in Acts 15) before this huge wall officially came down, and even then it wasn't easy. They weren't talking about the color of the carpet. Or whether to pave the parking lot. They were trying to decide if the doors of the church should be open to Gentiles as well as to Jews, or if converts had to become Jewish and submit to all the Jewish laws and customs before they could become Christian.

Thank God the Holy Spirit saw to it that the doors of the church were swung wide open to accommodate all men and women of all races and nationalities and tongues! The God of Heaven was thundering from his majestic throne: The church is no place for walls! Tear them down, and as you open your doors, open your hearts to receive everyone who by faith comes through! My kingdom is no place for walls!

Listen to the exultation, the joy, in the voice of the Apostle Paul as he shouts the good news that Christ "himself is our peace," that Christ has "destroyed the barrier, the dividing wall of hostility" between Gentile and Jew (Ephesians 2:14)! And then extend that blessed truth all the way from east to west, to slave and free, male and female, Baptist and Church of Christ, Republican and Democrat. The walls are down!

"He came," Paul affirms, "to preach peace to you who were far away and peace to those who are near" (2:17). To chisel away the mortar of hate and tear down walls of hostility. To build instead the glorious church of God with love itself as the mortar and Christ as the chief cornerstone.

"And," Paul says, "in him you too"—and I hear him saying, you who are rich or poor, male or female, black or white, young or old: everyone standing together on the level ground at the foot of the cross and through faith accepting that sacrifice—"are being built together to become a dwelling in which God lives by his Spirit" (2:22).

How to Measure a Rainbow

The walls are down and the temple reaches to Heaven. It happened because of a cross.

And because of a cross it can happen today.

Joe Maxwell tells the story of how on a cool October evening in Mississippi he watched a cross go up. Not that long ago in our nation's history it might have been raised by men in white hoods and lit with torches, brightly-flaming evidence of racial hatred in a state which has witnessed over 700 lynchings.

But not this time. This cross-raising reminded Maxwell of the "famed scene on Iwo Jima" as soldiers struggled to raise our flag. This time, "black hands on white on black," a "mass of coated-and-tied men straining against their common history" of distrust and hatred, raised "a symbol of new life on Mississippi soil."

Twenty-four thousand Christians, black and white, were coming together in the Deep South to celebrate the new unity they felt after a year of actively working to tear down the wall between races, to foster black and white friendships one on one, couple with couple, church with church. To beat racism one friendship at a time.[10]

After a year of hard work—eating together, working together, praying together—they came together to celebrate what unites them—the cross of Christ. It was that cross they lifted up.

Together.

That cross tears down walls.

Walls come down when black men and white men acknowledge their common humanity and the deep need they share, the need for a Savior.

Walls come down when fathers hug their teenage sons and focus on what unites them rather than on what divides.

A Hole in the Wall

Walls come down when Christians from all over town from all sorts of traditions come together to praise God for the Savior they mutually extol as their only reason for hope and their best reason for thanksgiving.

Through the cross of Christ, walls come down.

Need a wall torn down?

Take my advice. Call an expert.

Chapter 5

For this reason I, Paul, the prisoner of Christ Jesus for the sake of you Gentiles—

Surely you have heard about the administration of God's grace that was given to me for you, that is, the mystery made known to me by revelation, as I have already written briefly. In reading this, then, you will be able to understand my insight into the mystery of Christ, which was not made known to men in other generations as it has now been revealed by the Spirit to God's holy apostles and prophets. This mystery is that through the gospel the Gentiles are heirs together with Israel, members together of one body, and sharers together in the promise in Christ Jesus.

I became a servant of this gospel by the gift of God's grace given me through the working of his power. Although I am less than the least of all God's people, this grace was given me: to preach to the Gentiles the unsearchable riches of Christ, and to make plain to everyone the administration of this mystery, which for ages past was kept hidden in God, who created all things. His intent was that now, through the church, the manifold wisdom of God should be made known to the rulers and authorities in the heavenly realms, according to his eternal purpose which he accomplished in Christ Jesus our Lord. In him and through faith in him we may approach God with freedom and confidence. I ask you, therefore, not to be discouraged because of my sufferings for you, which are your glory.

Ephesians 3:1-13

Paint Creek &
The Mystery of Christ

. . . you will be able to understand my insight into the mystery of Christ,
which was not made known to men in other generations
as it has now been revealed by the Spirit
to God's holy apostles and prophets.
EPHESIANS 3:4-5

My younger brother Jim and I walked among the headstones dotting the small country cemetery nestled near the Edith Community a little over eight miles outside of Robert Lee, Texas.

Strange that the names of creeks would so distinguish dry West Texas.

Yellow Wolf Creek.

Messbox Creek.

Rough Creek.

Well-kept but absolutely blending in with their surroundings, the headstones at Paint Creek Cemetery had grown up where once only mesquite trees and prickly pears had dotted the landscape. Not far off, but far enough away to be absolutely unobtrusive, was a defunct country cafe and a flock of goats.

A few jackrabbits darted in and out between the stones, oblivious to the mute but powerful witness borne by granite markers to untold stories and the fabric of life and love, tragedy and triumph, joy and sadness laid out before us in the patchwork quilt of humanity's struggle.

Jim and I walked, talked, and wondered about the stories.

Just a little way over from where we were standing was a

93

short white stone, a little granite lamb resting on its top, bearing the names of three boys, triplets we supposed—Terry, Kerry, and Gerry—and only one date.

Date of birth.

Date of death.

The same.

Not far away was a larger stone bearing two names—Arizona Cain Robertson and Maurice Robertson. Mother and child. The date of her death was the date of the birth, and the death, of her child. And it pointed to another death.

A death of dreams.

Her dreams, of course. But also the dreams of a husband/father as on that May day in 1928 the sun of his deepest joy was unexpectedly eclipsed by the darkness of an even deeper sadness.

Many of the stones bore witness to conflict. One stone honored a 1st Sergeant who fought with Company E of the 2nd Texas Regiment, Confederate States Army. Another was a memorial to a **"Private, World War I, 31st Division, Company 165, Depot Brigade."**

Many stones. Many battles.

With life. With death.

I wondered about a three-year-old. **"1925-1928. ONLY SLEEPING."**

I wondered about the perky-looking 32-year-old whose photograph watched me from her headstone.

I wondered about the stories.

More than a few of the names in that country cemetery I recognized. Names of Robert Lee families. Harmon. Bruton. Boykin. King. Peay.

And names like Key and Shropshire. Both strains of blood run in my veins.

And Shelburne.

The first time I ever saw that name chiseled on a headstone, it caught me by surprise. Still makes me feel funny.

It shouldn't.

Alf Key, my great-grandfather, donated land for that cemetery. His bones lie there. Not much more than a stone's throw from the windmill and remaining ruins of his old homestead.

As do D. P. Key's, his son and my granddad.

And Wilma Shelburne's, D. P.'s daughter. My mother.

The pattern on the quilt is emerging. Death hasn't skipped a single generation. And it won't skip mine.[1]

But the Author of Life will have the last word in the story.

Alf Key had no idea what he was setting in motion back in 1888 when he and his wife Cornelia homesteaded in Coke County, Texas.

Alf Key was born in 1865, the year the American Civil War ended. On Sunday, April 9, 1865, Generals Robert E. Lee and Ulysses S. Grant met at Appomattox, Virginia, and Lee surrendered. On Friday, April 14, President Abraham Lincoln was assassinated at Ford's Theatre. And earlier that week, on Monday, April 10, Alf Key was born.

Alf died in 1956. Less than a year before I was born.

It's ironic, you know. He and I have spent many a night in the same old house in Robert Lee. But we never spent a single moment together.

He loved more than a few of the same people I have loved.

His thoughts and attitudes and actions, the choices he made in his life, affect me every day of my life in ways that I cannot begin to imagine. But I wonder.

Do I have his eyes? His hair? His tone or timbre of voice?

More important than his eyes, do I have his vision?

How much of the way I see the world is colored by the way he saw the world?

I wonder. And I'll bet he wondered, too, though he never knew my name. I'll bet he wondered about what he was setting in motion.

Did he ever pick up a stone from the red Coke County ground, toss it into a pool of water in Paint Creek, watch the ripples, and wonder about the people, the names, the faces, the lives that would be the ripples set in motion by his life?

Alf Key knew from whence he'd come. He knew the kind of values he was trying to instill in his children. He lived a long 90 years, long enough to see the fruit that was coming from roots he'd worked to nurture.

He'd done what he needed to do to help set the plot in motion. Now his kids and grandkids were writing or beginning to write their own chapters in the story. He could only guess what chapters they might write with their lives.

Alf Key's chapter was ending on one side of the page and mine was beginning on the other. That this old gentleman I never knew could affect me so profoundly is a mystery to me. And I wonder about the lives I'm affecting, shaping, coloring right now.

But I can't read that far ahead.

Only the true Author knows about the lives on the other side of the page. Only he knows what will be written there. Only he knows when it's time to turn the page.

My great-grandfather didn't look much like an Old Testament patriarch or prophet. (He had a magnificent moustache but sported no beard to go with it.) But, in a small way, he shared their dilemma. He knew he was part of a story, but how the pages would turn and the plot would unfold, he didn't know.

Neither did they.

Nowhere in the Old Testament will you find a man more committed to God, more used by him, more a part of the divine plan that would culminate in the cross and the resurrection than the one-time slave baby, one-time prince, one-time shepherd named Moses.

We read the wonderful story of Moses' life quickly. But don't you know that as Moses lived it, he often wondered about the story being written?

I wonder . . .

A Shepherd's Story

All taken together, it was not that bad a life, the shepherd mused, guiding his sheep toward the well. The work could be hard, but he was not afraid to bend his back. It was honest work, was it not?

And the sheep he governed? Well, they were sheep!

Leave courage to lions, cunning to tigers, antics to monkeys, and wisdom to owls. Sheep make no great claim to any of those attributes. They were just like any "run of the mill" animal, his shepherd friends might have mused, only more so!

More likely to get themselves into the sort of fix it took a wary shepherd to rectify, but more likely to get under your skin with that simple trust they placed in a loving shepherd.

More likely to wander off and get lost, but more of a joy to find, too.

More likely to need extra attention right at the times you were busiest, but, he figured, maybe more likely to deserve it.

No, he didn't mind taking care of sheep. After all, it had been misguidedly taking care of people, not sheep, that had nearly done him in so many years ago.

How to Measure a Rainbow

It almost seemed now like it had been another lifetime.

When he had come here to Midian—it was more accurate to say, when he had *run* here to Midian—he was running for his life. He'd looked for all the world like the Egyptian prince that he was, the adopted son of Pharaoh's daughter.

But that was a very long time ago.

No one would take him for a prince of Egypt now. He was a shepherd, and he looked the part. He'd traded a scepter for a shepherd's staff. His only subjects were the sheep under his care. Let other men rule kingdoms. Keeping his sheep out of harm's way was challenge enough for him.

Well, he'd been lost in thought long enough, sitting on a hillock of grass watching his sheep graze. As he stood, it occurred to him that he was content with his life in Midian, that he liked his shepherd's work and, not least, he liked the time he spent out on the hills far away from others—quiet time, time to think, to ponder, to wonder.

He could live and die a shepherd and that would be fine with him. But he wondered why the God of his fathers had chosen for him such a circuitous route to Midian?

Why have him born in a foreign land, a land of slavery in which his first breath might well have been his last?

Why have him floated down river in a basket and plucked from the arms of the Nile to become an Egyptian prince?

Why let him be chased out of Egypt when his own sense of who he was as a Hebrew flared into deadly force?

Surely, Lord, there is a quicker way to put a man in Midian to serve as a shepherd!

No, he didn't understand the Providence that had guided his life. But he knew that now he was a shepherd, and that was enough. And he knew that the sheep straying over toward the south side of the hill needed his care more than he needed to ponder.

Hmm. Looks like something's burning behind that hill. I wonder . . .[2]

God's people have always wondered. Even the men and women of greatest faith have wondered.

About what he's up to.

About what he would do.

About where he would lead.

In their lives. In the lives of their people. In the story being written in this world.

From the time of the fall to sin in the Garden, the Author of Life began hinting at, pointing toward, foreshadowing, the wonderful climax of his story.

I suppose the first hint is given way back in Genesis 3 where God hints to a snakebitten world that the time would come when the serpent's head would be crushed by the Seed of woman.

Many years later God's word is given to Abraham that through the old patriarch and his children all the nations of the earth would one day be blessed.

Don't you know Abraham wondered what that meant!

God was telling him about a marvelous story that would be—was already being—written, and Abraham and his kids were being cast in leading roles.

But wait! Kids?

When the promise was given, old—very old—Abraham didn't even have one child.

How are you going to write a story and feature a family if the family in question is just a childless husband and wife?

How are you going to write a story of epic proportions if the main character's likely to die childless somewhere in the next paragraph? (No insurance underwriter in his right mind would write a policy on a man that old!)

But the Author had a marvelous plot twist in mind.

By the time of the prophets, God scatters even more hints that the time would not be long. The Messiah, the one who would save God's people, was coming!

To a people oppressed by their enemies, a people who had been held captive by one foreign king after another, a people who desperately needed a reason to hope, a nation the pages of whose history had been blotched with blood and tears, the Author pointed to the time when he would break into the story in a marvelous way.

The people heard, and they wondered.

And well they might. I would have wondered, too. And I never could have guessed the story the Author of Heaven would write.

Think about it. Does God ever do anything just like we'd expect him to?

A world to save,

a Gift to give,

a Baby to send.

And the greatest Christmas Present ever given is all wrapped up in swaddling cloths and laid in a feed trough.

And the mother of the King is a poor Jewish girl whose wedding, the thin-lipped gossips around Bethlehem would be quick to tell you, was much less than a discreet nine months before the birth. Mark it down, those gals could count to nine just as quickly as their modern counterparts.

And the birth announcement for God's Son? It was proclaimed by angels whose glory split the skies, but ("who'd-a-thunk-it?") the amazing proclamation was not made at a grand meeting of pompously assembled and well-robed religious moguls of the Judean Diocese or the Southern Palestinian

Convention or the Greater Bethlehem Ministerial Association.

No, it was proclaimed to terrified shepherds whose collars, if they'd had such, would have been decidedly blue, whose theology, if you could call it that, had more to do with the ancient equivalent of Starr Cut Plug tobacco than it did with heavenly lights. These were simple and rough-hewn men who'd spent lots of time on hills herding sheep and precious little time at all in synagogues.

They'd seen angels? Yeah, right. The folks back in town knew full well that the last time old Issachar had seen an angel he'd found him at the bottom of a wineskin.

But not this time.

Oh, some of them had been a bit sleepy just a moment before, but that had changed in a heartbeat, in the blink of an eye, as the night sky exploded with light and angels ripped apart the firmament to emblazon Heaven's message across the shimmering sky.

God's promise of salvation and the coming of the great King had been made long centuries before. Generations of kings had come and gone. And generations of shepherds had kept watch over their sheep on these same hills while Bethlehem slept below and, slumbering uneasily with the little city, a careworn world waited for God to rouse it with good news.

But then the message of Heaven came. The message of your salvation and mine. And it came to shepherds.

Who'd a thunk it?

God Writes a Mystery

You see, the story that God has been writing down through the centuries is a mystery. Always has been. His people who know him, who love him, and who are loved by him, have always wondered what he would write next.

He has always surprised us. At every turn of the page.

But the twists in the plot have always been far more wonderful than we could ever have written ourselves or even imagined.

Paul writes to the Ephesians about the "mystery of Christ," the mystery that many had longed to unravel, the mystery "now . . . revealed by the Spirit to God's holy apostles" (3:5).

It's the mystery that through the Good News of God, Gentiles and Jews would stand together as heirs of the promise in Christ.

It's the mystery unfolding in the church as all of Heaven watches amazed at the way God is accomplishing his purpose in the universe.

One mystery, you see, stands behind it all.

"My Son . . ."

The Father's words boomed like thunder in Heaven's throne room and rolled down steps of ethereal alabaster through the Great Hall of Glory and out into Eternity.

The heavenly host heard not the words, but the mighty music of the voice of God flooded through Heaven's streets, every magnificent reverberation joining the great rolling stream, each wondrous wave capped with divine overtones of the Father's love. And on earth, thunder.

"My Son, everything I have is yours. Nothing have I withheld. You are clothed in heavenly splendor. To you has been granted glory which knows no bounds.

"From before the foundations of the earth, before Eternity at my command whispered, 'Time!' and my Spirit brooded over an incubating creation, I have loved you.

"You who are clothed with me in the timeless splendor of Heaven.

How to Measure a Rainbow

"You who are Light and Love and all Beauty, and the Joy of your Father.

"Now, in the Eternal Present where every moment is now, I ask, will you willingly enter time? Will you allow your divinity to be wrapped in the garment of humanity? Will you lay aside heavenly glory to redeem the fallen sons of Adam and daughters of Eve?"

In Heaven, where every moment is now, the Son's voice now. "*Abba*, Father, Thy will be done."

And Heaven, now hearing, gasped, and through the timeless Hall echoed the sounds of an angel's voice hailing the handmaid of God,

the gentle sound of the Baby's first breath and the sharp birth
cry filling a Bethlehem stable,
the Father's mighty thunder of approval—"This is my
beloved Son, in whom I am well pleased!",[3]
the sharp metallic sounds of a soldier's hammer eclips
ing the Son on a tree,
Heaven's verdict—"It is finished,"[4]
and the Son's—"Father, into thy hands I
commit my spirit."[5]

All of these chords intermingle with the angel's eternal message, "He is not here! He is risen!"[6]

And Heaven gasped.

And angels, numbering ten thousands times ten thousands, sang with tongues of light:
"Worthy is the Lamb, who
was slain,
to receive power and wealth
and wisdom and
strength and honor
and glory and
praise!"[7]
Worthy is the Lamb!

You may wonder what God, the great Author, is writing in the story of your life.

Alf Key wondered. And Moses long before him. And shepherds standing out on Judean hills two thousand years ago. And two minutes ago.

And you. And me.

Don't worry. You're loved by the Author. He's got a great ending in mind which is really not an ending at all. It's by far the most beautiful of all beautiful beginnings, and it will never end.

You see, love is the last word—and the first word—in the story because the Author "is love."[8]

And he loves you.

Chapter 6

For this reason I kneel before the Father, from whom his
whole family in heaven and on earth derives its name.
I pray that out of his glorious riches he may strengthen you
with power through his Spirit in your inner being, so that Christ
may dwell in your hearts through faith. And I pray that you,
being rooted and established in love, may have power, together
with all the saints, to grasp how wide and long and high and
deep is the love of Christ, and to know this love that surpasses
knowledge—that you may be filled to the measure of all the
fullness of God.
Now to him who is able to do immeasurably more than all
we ask or imagine, according to his power that is at work within
us, to him be glory in the church and in Christ Jesus throughout
all generations, for ever and ever! Amen.

Ephesians 3:14-21

How To Measure
a Rainbow

I pray that you . . . may have power . . .
to grasp how wide and long and high and deep
is the love of Christ, . . .
EPHESIANS 3:17-18

E ver try to measure a rainbow? Has it ever occurred to
you as you gazed across the horizon after a life-giving
rain and saw emblazoned across God's vast sky the
beautiful palette of the Creator's color, that maybe you should
take a trip to the end of the rainbow? Not to try to find a pot of
gold. No, to begin instead, tape measure in hand, the serious
business of measuring that beautiful bow from one end to the
other?

I doubt it. As far as I know, nobody has ever tried, but I'm
surprised! We try to measure everything else!

I read once about a group of scientists who decided to
weigh a man before death, and then immediately after, to try to
discover the weight of the human soul. You might as well try to
measure a rainbow.

In this life, there is a time for cold calculation and methodi-
cal measurement, but some things were never meant to be
measured, only experienced.

How many of you fathers have ever been tempted to take
calculator in hand to figure the economic value of the hugs of
your giggling three-year-old daughter? You might as well try to
measure a rainbow.

How could you put a price tag on the feeling you get when

you read the note from one of your Little Leaguers' moms: "Dear Coach, we are so thankful Jordan was lucky enough to have you for a coach"? You might as well try to measure a rainbow.

Ever look up on a starlit night and experience an almost irresistible longing to count the number of the stars in the sky before marveling at their beauty? You'd have about as much luck measuring a rainbow.

It makes about as much sense to put up a ladder to try to take a lick of the Milky Way. That's a lot like trying to measure a rainbow.

Ever try to measure a rainbow?

It won't take you long to find out that it can't be done. But lots of us would like to try.

We like to talk in quantitative terms. About size. Depth. Height. Breadth. About value. About worth. Too often the measurements we use are all in dollars and cents.

We're folks, after all, who like to see things in black and white. Bottom line folks. Grownup folks.

Grownup folks are okay. We have our strengths. But too often we also have a serious handicap. Too often, somewhere after we grew up, our sense of wonder and awe and imagination atrophied as our bodies grew and our minds began to measure life itself only in terms of gross national product, consumer price indexes, and taxable income.

Too often our bottom line mentality is betrayed by our language. Most ten-year-olds still have imaginations that haven't withered. Forty-year-olds may size each other up by remarking, "I wonder what he's worth?" They have a hard time seeing past bank balances.

Not ten-year-olds.

Ten-year-olds know more about net worth. They don't judge their friends by weighing their piggy banks. Who cares?

Ten-year-olds know what's really important.

How to Measure a Rainbow

Like who's the best at catching lizards.

Or who has the best ideas for tree houses and clubs.

Or who's a friend you can count on when the going gets tough and the class bully's coming around the corner.

It's adults who get all caught up in such trivia as who's got the biggest house or the shiniest car or the healthiest savings account. Ten-year-olds are better off. They've still got their imaginations and a God-given talent for squeezing the juice out of every bit of life's fruit.

And that'll beat a savings account any day!

They've got time to thank God for rainbows by experiencing their beauty and not getting hung up about what a rainbow's worth in dollars and cents. Some adults do, too, but not nearly enough.

Astronaut and Wonder-watcher

Do you remember Scott Carpenter?

Scott Carpenter was one of the original Mercury Seven astronauts in a time when "astronaut" was a word that had just been coined. Carpenter was one of the seven chosen, after an unbelievably rigorous process, to be one of the first fellows launched off into space atop a huge fire-belching Roman candle filled up with tons of highly explosive fuel. It took a special breed to do that job.

Carpenter had what it took. The "right stuff."

Scott Carpenter was a test pilot.

He knew all about tests and data dealing with speed and trajectory and detailed specifications.

He knew how to read gauges and fiddle with gadgets and record the kinds of facts that earth-bound engineers and technicians would hover over for hours on end.

But, according to astronauts Deke Slayton and Alan Shepard

in their book *Moon Shot,* woven through the fabric that made up Scott Carpenter was a strand of poetry.[1] Along with Carpenter's ability to do the technical astronaut stuff was a very well-developed sense of wonder.

Carpenter followed Alan Shepard, the first American in space; Gus Grissom, the second; and John Glenn, the first American to orbit the earth. He was the fourth American to fly past the wild blue yonder and into space, and the second to orbit the globe.

Shepard's ride was almost perfect. Grissom's and Glenn's both had their scary moments, but on the whole went very well indeed.

But Carpenter had a bit of a problem.

It wasn't a problem with the rocket or the capsule or any of the technology.

You could say, I suppose, that if an astronaut happened to come across a rainbow on his way to the moon, NASA wanted it measured.

Carpenter, the astronaut with poet's blood, wasn't interested in measuring rainbows. To extend the metaphor, if Carpenter could have reached out and caught a rainbow, a scientist might have gotten his jollies from running tests on a rainbow thus retrieved. An engineer might get absolutely giddy over a device he'd come up with to suck up rainbows. But Carpenter felt that rainbows weren't meant to be measured, just experienced.

As Scott Carpenter flew his craft orbiting our globe, he found himself almost lost in the wonder of it all. He was busy looking outward to marvel at the beauties of his universe and just as busy looking inward to his own soul and cataloging the effect of the wonder.

NASA was interested in measuring the levels of solar radiation; Carpenter found himself measuring the levels of wonder in his own soul.

How to Measure a Rainbow

He was almost overdosing on wonder when he discovered that he was three minutes late. Wonder-watchers, after all, don't make the best clock-watchers.

He was three minutes late firing the rockets that needed to be fired to adjust his course for re-entry. And then it was time to fire them for sure. But he was out of fuel. To get down safely now, without literally burning up, would be a trick to challenge the nerve of any test pilot.

If re-entry didn't kill him, the fellows on the ground would.

Scott Carpenter made it down safely. (So what if it was the wrong ocean? Just kidding.[2])

Unfortunately, he'd rubbed the brass the wrong way. They'd wanted rainbows measured, not experienced. Like his colleagues before, he received a hero's welcome home. But his first trip into space was his last.

If there was a rainbow up there, NASA wanted it measured.

I suppose I see NASA's point of view. But I like Carpenter's better.

A Time To Put Tape Measures Away

Some things simply can't be adequately quantified and measured. The time comes when we'd best put the tape measures away and learn the truth that some things can only be felt and savored.

I think that truth partly accounts for the beautiful section of praise Paul drops into the middle of his great *Letter to the Ephesians*.

All through the letter he's praising God for, as he puts it, bringing "all things in heaven and on earth together under one head," Jesus Christ (1:10).

It's through Christ that the world has meaning and we have direction.

How to Measure a Rainbow

It's through Christ that you and I were chosen to be the very children of God.

It's through Christ that Gentile and Jew, slave and free, black and white, rich and poor, all come to God on the level ground at the foot of the cross and are accepted on the very same basis, that of grace.

It's through Christ that the barrier, the wall, between God and man, Gentile and Jew, slave and free has been knocked down and we rise up together, one people united in Christ, to praise God for his mercy.

It's through Christ and his blood that we have pardon.

It's through Christ and his resurrection that we have power.

It's through Christ, Paul writes, that he himself, the "least of all God's people," was given the grace to preach the gospel to the Gentiles (3:8).

It's through Christ that "rulers and authorities in heavenly realms," and, indeed, the whole universe look on in wonder and amazement as the eternal purpose of God unfolds on this little globe (3:10).

And it is through Christ that the King of the Universe invites us, you and me, to "approach God with freedom and confidence" (3:12).

All of these truths pass before Paul like the stardust in the tail of a comet and the reality itself, the bright ball of fire that makes it all possible, is the power of God at work on a cross.

"My God, my God, why have you forsaken me?" Jesus cried in pain as he hung on the cross and felt the weight of our sin and the separation from his Father.[3]

But it's because of that cross that Paul now cries in utter joy and exultation, "My God, my God, how can we possibly praise you enough for loving us so deeply and so much!"

As Paul stands before the rainbow of God's love, it's not a time for measurement and calculation, though Paul had a flare for that. Who better to set forth the doctrine and theology that undergirds our faith than Paul in Romans as he parries and thrusts and puts away the arguments of detractors who would throw away the good news of salvation through grace for the bad news of damnation through law?

Paul could wield the sword of logic with the best of them. And all of his rational thought and the beautiful logic of God's plan are still very much in place, still true. But now's not the time for that.

You don't stand before the Milky Way with a paper cup trying to catch stardust.

You don't start counting the rings on a redwood calculating how many fences it would build before you stand back and just say "Wow!" to the wonder of that kind of creative majesty.

You don't stand looking across Niagara Falls proud as punch that mankind knows how to harness hydroelectric power. You stand back amazed at a God powerful enough to create such magnificent beauty, a God who never saw a day when his simplest wisdom didn't dwarf our highest thought.

Paul stands in the gallery with the angels and the whole universe watching in amazement as the plan of God unfolds. The rainbow of God's love stretches from one end of the sky to the other lit up by the rich colors of divine mercy and grace.

No one has to tell Paul that this is not a time to measure rainbows. In absolute awe he falls to his knees almost overdosing on the sheer wonder of God's power and God's love.

"For this reason I kneel before the Father . . ."

Paul kneels before the God who gives us all, black and white, rich and poor, Gentile and Jew, his name. He falls down before the God who out of the boundless riches of his grace has chosen paupers like us to be King's kids. And he prays for our strength.

Not for our strength to somehow achieve salvation by our own merit.

Not for our ability to spiritually "pull ourselves up by our own bootstraps."

Not for our intellectual prowess that we'd be smart enough to understand absolutely correctly every "jot and tittle" of doctrine and get God all figured out.

No, Paul's prayer is more focused than that. It's a narrower beam pointing to a much more wonderful request which, if granted, will open up every part of our lives to God's light.

The great apostle looks out across the magnificent rainbow of God's love and his prayer for the Ephesians, and for you and me, is this—that we will have the power to begin to see the wonder of God's love.

> I pray that you, being rooted and established in love, may have power together with all the saints, to grasp how wide and long and high and deep is the love of Christ, and to know that this love surpasses knowledge—that you may be filled to the measure with all the fullness of God (3:17b-19).

God's love is so great that it can never be fully measured, but, wonder of wonders, it can be experienced!

Ever try to measure a rainbow? No hardware store makes a measuring tape long enough. How could we begin to measure the love of God?

How do you use a calculator to fix a price for love? How do you put a price on the kind of love that would cause the Master of the Universe to leave the royal robes of divinity in Heaven and to take up the poor garment of humanity?

How do you measure a rainbow? How indeed!

How do you begin to measure God's love to this world?

Maybe more to the point, how do you personally begin to measure his love to you? How do I?

What's it worth in dollars and cents that God gave me

parents whose love was always as certain and constant as my next breath?

For that matter, how could I put a monetary value on breath itself, God's gift of life?

What would I write on the price tag for the love and friendship of the wife whose constant support has been for me as steadfast and trustworthy as the rotation of Planet Earth?

What's it worth to have sons who love me and make me proud, brothers who've been for me friends and mentors, a sister (and some neat sisters-in-law) whose estimation of me is way out of line, and friends who've been as close as family? How do you put a price tag on that kind of blessing?

What's it worth to have the opportunity to preach the good news of God's grace to a church that really believes it and is serious about acting it out in love?

How do you measure a rainbow?

You don't.

You treasure the experience.

You bask in its beauty.

And as feeble as our human attempts may be, you resolve to lend your voice to the music of the spheres and thank God with every breath for the rainbow of his love.

Do You See Rainbows or Do You See Rain?

I think Max Lucado probably has us pegged when he says that "In any given Christian community there are two groups: those who are contagious in their joy and those who are cranky in their faith. They've accepted Christ and are seeking him, but their balloon has no helium. One is grateful, the other is grumpy. Both are saved. Both are heaven bound. But one sees the rainbow and the other sees the rain."[4]

How to Measure a Rainbow

Look for the rainbow of God's love. As wonder blends with gratitude, you will notice that every breath brings new reasons to thank God for his love—sometimes in some situations that may surprise you!

It was getting on toward midnight several weeks ago, and I was driving home after visiting one of our members who was seriously ill in a large hospital some seventy miles from our town. Micro-cassette tape recorder in hand, I was trying to snatch some writing time in a week where that kind of time had been scarce. As I rolled down the highway musing aloud to my tape recorder about "measuring rainbows," I had a multicolored experience of another sort that is guaranteed to get anyone's head right out of the clouds.

Yes, indeed, I saw colors!

Red. Blue. Bright orange now, too. (That one surprised me.) And the cab of my pickup lit up with brilliant white light.

You may think it was some UFO experience with extraterrestrials. No. It was Marty Johnson, State Trooper.[5]

That settled me down a bit. Rainbows may shimmer at the speed of light, but pickup trucks and preachers better cruise closer to the speed limit.

But later, as I pulled back onto the road, it occurred to me how far down God's love reaches to each of us every day in amazingly practical ways. As Lloyd John Ogilvie has written, seen from this perspective, every bush becomes a burning bush, every seemingly mundane experience a holy experience transformed by God's presence.[6]

I found myself thankful to live in a community where I can call the highway patrol officer by his first name and laugh with him while he's writing the warning ticket. (Yes, it was only a warning! If that's not God's grace at work, I don't know what is—and you don't know Marty!)

I'm thankful that the reflections of God's love, glimmers of the rainbow, come to us every day in every way if we just open our eyes to the wonder.

This week, as your three-year-old gives you a hug, a coworker gets you coffee, your spouse gives you a kiss, and God gives you a sunrise, look for reflections of God's love, and I'll bet you'll start to see them behind every corner.

When they come, don't worry about measuring the rainbow. Just give thanks for it!

Chapter 7

As a prisoner for the Lord, then, I urge you to live a life worthy of the calling you have received. Be completely humble and gentle; be patient, bearing with one another in love. Make every effort to keep the unity of the Spirit through the bond of peace. There is one body and one Spirit—just as you were called to one hope when you were called—one Lord, one faith, one baptism; one God and Father of all, who is over all and through all and in all.

But to each one of us grace has been given as Christ apportioned it. This is why it says:

"When he ascended on high,
he led captives in his train
and gave gifts to men."

(What does "he ascended" mean except that he also descended to the lower, earthly regions? He who descended is the very one who ascended higher than all the heavens, in order to fill the whole universe.) It was he who gave some to be apostles, some to be prophets, some to be evangelists, and some to be pastors and teachers, to prepare God's people for works of service, so that the body of Christ may be built up until we all reach unity in the faith and in the knowledge of the Son of God and become mature, attaining to the whole measure of the fullness of Christ.

Then we will no longer be infants, tossed back and forth by the waves, and blown here and there by every wind of teaching and by the cunning and craftiness of men in their deceitful scheming. Instead, speaking the truth in love, we will in all things grow up into him who is the Head, that is, Christ. From him the whole body, joined and held together by every supporting ligament, grows and builds itself up in love, as each part does its work.

Ephesians 4:1-16

Running on
the Right Road

*. . . so that the body of Christ may be built up
until we all reach unity in the faith and in the knowledge
of the Son of God and become mature, . . .*
EPHESIANS 4:12-13

I love snow. I suppose I've always loved the white stuff. Some of my fondest memories of childhood have to do with snowy days at home in Amarillo, Texas. Were the snows there really as deep as I remember? Was I just a lot smaller? Both?

We got great snows in Amarillo. I remember drifts piled high, all the way up to the window of the bedroom my younger brother and I shared. Jim and I soon discovered that opening the window and diving out of the house headlong down the natural snowslide was loads of fun! And I remember one particularly heavy snow when the drifts on each side of our shoveled sidewalk towered a good bit higher than my head. I loved it!

I had a love affair with snow even before I had the wheels and the opportunity to feel that particular joy that comes from crafting a perfect "donut" in the pristine, unmarked snow of an inviting parking lot.

I still love snow (and don't broadcast this—I still do donuts), but for years I've found myself longing for a really good one, a snow like the ones I remember from my childhood. The snows in our little town have been pretty wimpy for the last few years. And one of the problems with growing up is that as we get bigger and taller it takes bigger snows to be as impressive as were the big ones when we were kids.

How to Measure a Rainbow

But we recently had a very impressive snow. A fine snow. A big snow by anybody's standards. Most of the snow showed up on a Friday evening. (I'll tell you more about that in a moment.) Saturday morning we woke up absolutely blanketed under the beautiful stuff. Right after lunch a bunch of our church folks and some fine representatives from our neighborhood met at the local elementary school. Big playground. Lots of snow. We had the best snowball fight ever! (Thirty-and-over-year-olds against under-thirty-year-olds. The older folks won, you see, largely because they took the time to count "hits" while the younger folks were too busy throwing snowballs to tally up the ones that were connecting!)

Deliciously tired, my family and I trudged back up the hill to our house. I took one look at the yard. So much snow. So little time. Wonderful wet snow, perfect stuff for snowballs or snow-anythings, so . . . Joshua, our youngest son, and I flew right into some snow artistry. We built a snow dragon, spikes down the back, long twisting tail, knobby skin, proud head held high.

Late that night, I woke up (probably in need of Tylenol), tiptoed into the living room, and peeked out the window. The nighttime world was alive with the calm, beautiful, bluish-white glow of moonbeams on snow. The dragon sat on his haunches in our front yard as if calmly and quietly but strongly guarding our castle (or, at least, our *casa*). And I was reminded that the Giver of all good blessings, snows included, never sleeps. Not a dragon, he's the Lion of the tribe of Judah, the One who watches over our "coming and going," our winters and springs, our snows and our harvests, "both now and forevermore" (Psalm 121:8).

Looking out across that moonlit scene, dragon and all, I paused to thank God for joy, for beauty, for snow, for life here, and for the promise of life hereafter.

When the biggest part of the snow fell on that Friday, my family and I were thirty miles away from home. Along with a large contingent of our fellow citizens, we'd made the thirty-mile trip to help establish once and for all (or at least once and for all for this season) the absolute superiority of our high school basketball teams over the teams of the Cretans (just kidding) to the east. We'd met them on our own turf earlier in the season and dealt with them admirably, I thought, but there'd been a bit of a question (only in their minds, I assure you) about the clock and the final buzzer at the end of a very close game. The video tape vindicated us, but we wanted none of that this time. No questions. Just a massive avalanche-style victory. So there we sat, spooned into a very small gymnasium cheering on the good guys.

The Varsity Girls held up their end of the contest very well indeed. A decisive victory. The Varsity Boys were about to take the court for their own contest.

But the gents who suddenly showed up on the court carrying on quite a discussion were older, balding guys in suits and some fellows in uniform. Officials of one sort or another, school officials and police officers, from both communities.

Oops! I thought. Somebody's carried the contest outside the gym and we've had a battle of another sort. But I was wrong.

What they were discussing was the snow. As we had been sitting in the warm and certainly heated (in every sense) gym, massive amounts of snow had been falling. The cars, the trees, the roads, the world, it seemed, was covered with snow. White as far as you could see. But you couldn't see far! Visibility, the highway folks informed us, was zero. They wanted to close the highway, but half of our town was still thirty miles from home.

The assembled moguls were getting their heads together to decide what to do. Well, probably what we should have done was to listen to the weather forecast and not make the trip in the first place, but it really had been a deceptively nice afternoon, and the tight schedule really held little room for makeup games . . . And by this time, that cow was pretty much out of the barn anyway. Four periods of basketball were probably not going to make that much difference. Zero visibility is pretty much the bottom of the scale. So we played. (And we won big. Thanks for asking.)

Then we started digging. The cars were out there. We just had to find them. Brushed off, shoveled off, scraped off, the cars were finally queued up, and we headed home. A long series of lights, lined up end to end like a curving luminescent snake, stretched from the defeated village we were abandoning all the way back to the homeland. The snaky procession slithered and slid every inch of those thirty miles at speeds never more than 30 m.p.h. and generally closer to 5 m.p.h. But we arrived home. Victorious.

That was an interesting night. It occurred to me later that part of what I felt that night sprang from the unity of purpose that, along with the massive amounts of snow, enveloped the evening. We'd been united against a common foe, of course. We'd done the job. The athletes, well-trained and finely-tuned physically and mentally, had played their hearts out. The fans, most of them badly in need of even a smidgeon of the kind of exercise taking place before them, had clapped and cheered and hollered idiotic inanities (what fans do, you know), and we had won the victory. Then we'd lined up together to face the cold and the snow.

Together against zero visibility.

Together against winter's fiercest elements.

Together against a highway department who, though benevolent and wanting us home, thought we were crazy for having left in the first place and wanted to close the road.

We were together. We slid in behind the snow plow (provided by the highway department) and its flashing light, and it led the way. All the way home.

Together.

Running on the Right Road

What Jesus Wants for Us

That's what Jesus wants for his people, you know. He wants us to be together, united in love and hope, in faith and purpose, in direction and spirit. And Spirit.

You and I were in his heart and on his mind when he spoke to the Father: "I pray . . . for those who will believe in me . . . that all of them may be one. . . . May they be brought to complete unity" (John 17:20-21, 23).

That's what the Holy Spirit is still telling God's people through the words of the great apostle. Paul is physically imprisoned (under house arrest), but his spirit is in no way eclipsed as he points to the wonder of what God has done for his people and to the calling that we have received.

To be gentle.

To be patient.

To be loving.

To celebrate the One who makes us one.

Eugene Peterson in *The Message* paraphrases Paul's words in this way as the apostle urges us to "run on the road God has called us to travel":

> In light of all this, here's what I want you to do. While I'm locked up here, a prisoner for the Master, I want you to get out there and walk—better yet, run!—on the road God called you to travel. I don't want any of you sitting around on your hands. I don't want anyone strolling off, down some path that goes nowhere. And mark that you do this with humility and discipline—not in fits and starts, but steadily, pouring yourselves out for each other in acts of love, alert at noticing differences and quick at mending fences.
>
> You were all called to travel on the same road and in the same direction, so stay together, both outwardly and inwardly. You have one Master, one faith, one baptism, one God and Father of all, who rules over all, works through all, and is present in all. Everything you are and think and do is permeated with Oneness.[1]

So, united as one because of the One who loved us, our task is to "run on the road God called us to travel." God has called us. God has empowered us. God has given us the unity we need to have the strength for the task.

Unity is something God gives. It's a gift. A priceless gift bought by nothing less than the blood of God's Son and kept alive and vibrant by the power of his Spirit.

Paul's plea is not that Christians somehow create unity. We might as well try to create a sunrise. What he wants us to do is to keep it, honor it, cherish it. He wants us to realize what a priceless gift we've been given. He wants us to recognize the unity that already exists through God's Spirit.

That's not always easy. Paul was well aware that folks, Christian or not, sometimes fuss.

I don't have any idea what was causing friction, for example, between two Philippian gals named Euodia and Syntyche. I do know that the friction was real, and the resulting fire had created enough smoke that Paul recognized a real danger to the church. He singles those ladies out and entreats them to "make up your differences as Christians should" (Philippians 4:2, PHILLIPS).

Now, let's be kind here. Let's assume that both of these gals were fine Christian women who, on the whole, did much that was good for God's people in Philippi. But they have gone down in history simply as two women who fussed loudly and longly enough that their quarrel threatened the health of the church they both undoubtedly professed to love.

They fussed.

But did their quarrel ever erase the fact that they were both sisters in the Lord? No! Paul doesn't write, "Become sisters in Christ!" That would be nonsense; they already were, even when the fur was flying. He is saying, "Act like what you are—sisters in the Lord."

126

Running on the Right Road

I would be a fool if I thought I needed to somehow create brotherhood between my younger brother and myself. It's already there, given to us by our parents through no effort of our own. He is my brother, and most of the time I'm proud to claim him. (Then there was the time he tried to blow the top off the neighbor's fencepost . . .) But whether I claim him or not makes no difference at all as far as our physical brotherhood goes. We are brothers because we have the same parents. Jim and I cannot create brotherhood. What we can do is recognize and cherish it.

So, says Paul, can God's kids. We can recognize our essential unity with all who are God's children. We can cherish the unity Christ died to make a reality. We can celebrate the fact that we are members of one Body. If we want to be mature, and if we want to run well on the road God has called us to travel, we will.

God calls us to recognize and cherish unity and thus to grow in maturity. It seems a delightful paradox that with unity as one of the deepest and finest gifts made possible by Christ, the Giver absolutely delights in the variety and diversity of the other gifts he has given his people.

My wife and I just bought a limited edition print by the gifted artist, G. Harvey. I should mention that Juana and I are not in the habit of buying fine art on a regular basis. At this stage in our lives and in the life of our four-boys-with-one-in-college-and-three-with-car-insurance family, our annual art budget is pretty much dwarfed by such items as dental bills and tennis shoes.

We broke the budget to buy this print. If we can ever afford to frame it, it will hang in the heart of our home. Entitled, "The Blessing," it will be a blessing to our family.[2]

How to Measure a Rainbow

Depicted in the painting, in a turn of the century setting with city shops, a carriage, and gas streetlights as the background, two women have stopped to admire a new mother's baby. The print is a beautiful thing, signed and numbered, splashed with color and rich with the warmth that is such a trademark of this fine artist. Warm yellows and crimsons and deep lavenders spread across the painting. The silver glow of the street lights suffuses the scene. The colors spread all across the canvas, different colors each with a role to play, and each beautiful but far more beautiful together, united, than they could ever be apart.

In painting the beautiful picture of his church, the Master Artist chose the rich, deep hue of unity to tie the whole painting together, but with that beautiful color deftly brushed behind it all, he began to skillfully splash the canvas with such a diversity of color and stroke and texture as to take our breath away with its beauty.

Paul tells us plainly, as Peterson paraphrases, "[Being one] doesn't mean you should all look and speak and act the same. Out of the generosity of Christ, each of us is given his own gift."[3] So that the whole body is built up and blessed.

What an amazing body, the Body of Christ! To see part of its wonder, we need look no further than our own bodies. In their fine book, *Fearfully and Wonderfully Made*, Paul Brand and Philip Yancey quote from St. Augustine: "Men go abroad to wonder at the height of the mountains, at the huge waves of the sea, at the long courses of the rivers, at the vast compass of the ocean, at the circular motion of the stars; and they pass by themselves without wondering."[4]

Brand and Yancey, though, focus our eyes inward as they discuss the wonders of DNA. In its DNA, they write, "every cell possesses a genetic code so complete that the entire body could be reassembled from the information in any one of the body's cells."[5]

In fact, write the authors, our bodies *are* being reassembled every moment as old cells die and new ones are formed to replace them. As they point out, not one of us inhabits the same body he wore ten years ago. All of the cells except brain cells and nerve cells are entirely new. The human body, they write, "is more like a fountain than a sculpture: maintaining its shape, but constantly being renewed."[6] But because of the identical DNA locked within each cell, the body remains a unified whole.

According to Brand and Yancey, if the instructions imprinted on each DNA strand were written out, they would fill a thousand six-hundred page books![7]

But they are not written in books; they are written inside each of the hundred trillion cells in our bodies binding each cell with every other cell to work for the good of the whole body.

So it is with the Body of Christ:

> Just as the complete identity code of my body inheres in each individual cell, so also the reality of God permeates every cell in his Body, . . . I sense that bond when I meet strangers in India or Africa or California who share my loyalty to the Head; instantly we become brothers and sisters, fellow cells in Christ's Body. I share the ecstasy of community in a universal Body that includes every man and woman in whom God resides.[8]

What an amazing Body, given life itself and all good gifts from the Giver of all. One Lord, one God, one Father, but many, many gifts. And every one of them given so that we, and our brothers and sisters, God's church, can run with joy on the "road God has called us to travel."

As Paul pens *Ephesians*, he may be "imprisoned" under house arrest, but he sees far beyond the walls of his confinement. He sees what God has done for each of us, and he urges us to live our lives in light of God's calling, to celebrate the unity of God's Spirit, to accept and use for God's glory the rich gifts our God has given, so that we can grow up and be "like Christ in everything." The apostle wants us to be "fully mature adults, fully developed within and without, fully alive like Christ."[9]

Quite a few years ago now, my brothers and I began renovating my Grandmother and Granddaddy Key's old home down in Robert Lee, Texas. This old house in Coke County was much like the snows of my childhood in Amarillo: it seemed a lot bigger when I was smaller! But, for my siblings and myself, it was a very big part of our growing up years, though it's really not a large house at all.

Grandmother and Granddaddy had been gone for a long time when we began working to restore the old place. It was sadly in need of paint, and we were trying to answer that need in the interior of the almost ancient house when we came to an old doorway.

It was just an old doorway. Between the kitchen and the living room. But I remembered it so well!

Every morning Granddaddy would sit in the kitchen, just inside that door, in front of a little brown homemade stand with a radio perched on top. He sat there astride an old kitchen chair listening to the morning news, and he always held a fly swatter. I figured he might occasionally swat flies with it, but I was quite sure that he swatted grandkids with it—playfully. Every time one of us ventured through the door.

I never round that corner without halfway expecting to see Granddaddy sitting there.

I never navigate through that doorway without expecting to feel a swat in the tail section.

In that old doorway so filled with memories, my brothers and I found a treasure—such a treasure that only a barbarian would dream of painting over it. A treasure that we removed with care and committed to the keeping of one of the older brothers. A treasure that was, to us if to no one else, almost a holy thing.

It was the 1 X 2-inch doorjamb that ran from the floor to the ceiling. On that thin and ancient piece of wood, up and down the middle portion of its length, were old pencil marks, lines, and by each mark, a name.

You know what it was, don't you? You probably had one of these in your home or in your own grandparents' house. It was the growth chart for the grandkids. It was where they backed you up, put a book on your head, and drew the line to chart your growth over the past year.

Did you know that God's house has one of those, too? Yes, indeed, I'm certain it does because his is a house full of growing kids. Some of us are just little guys and gals. We back up to the doorjamb (this one is gold, you know), but before we turn around we see lots of marks. Way up on the jamb we see some names we recognize.

Like Paul.

And Peter.

And James.

And John.

But there's one mark at the very top, the tallest of all. And by that mark is written the name of Jesus. He's our elder Brother, you know. He's the biggest, the tallest, the most mature of all. He's the One who is the standard for growth in the whole house so that "in all things," in unity and maturity, "we will grow up into him" (4:15).

Jesus is so tall. I don't think our elder Brother would blame us if occasionally we're almost tempted to loose hope when we see how very big he is and how very small we are. But Christ is the One cheering us on. He and the Father, the best Father of all, know we've got a long way to go, but love mingles with pride in their eyes, and we hear the Father's voice, "My! Look how you've grown!"

Thank God for divine eyes which see, as Natalie Sleeth writes in her beautiful song, "Hymn of Promise,"

> In the bulb there is a flower;
> In the seed, an apple tree;
> In cocoons, a hidden promise;
> Butterflies will soon be free!
>
> In the cold and snow of winter
> There's a spring that waits to be
> Unrevealed until its season,
> Something God alone can see.[10]

God sees the growth. And he is the One who makes the growth possible because "his very breath and blood flow through us, nourishing us so that we will grow up healthy in God, robust in love."[11]

We finally made it home that snowy night. It was a long way to travel in the snow and ice. It was cold and slick and the roads were treacherous. Sometimes we wondered if we'd ever see the lights of home.

But we were on the right road.
Moving in the right direction.
Traveling together.
And we made it home.

Chapter 8

So I tell you this, and insist on it in the Lord, that you must no longer live as the Gentiles do, in the futility of their thinking. They are darkened in their understanding and separated from the life of God because of the ignorance that is in them due to the hardening of their hearts. Having lost all sensitivity, they have given themselves over to sensuality so as to indulge in every kind of impurity, with a continual lust for more.

You, however, did not come to know Christ that way. Surely you heard of him and were taught in him in accordance with the truth that is in Jesus. You were taught, with regard to your former way of life, to put off your old self, which is being corrupted by its deceitful desires; to be made new in the attitude of your minds; and to put on the new self, created to be like God in true righteousness and holiness.

Ephesians 4:17-24

A Dragon's Tale

You were taught . . . to put off your old self,
which is being corrupted, . . . and to put on your new self,
created to be like God. . . .
EPHESIANS 4:22, 24

S ome of the deepest and truest truths are best learned and experienced through the power of story. And some of the best stories are fantasies.

They couldn't happen in the real world, you know. Except that the truths they contain "happen" in our world in one way or another every day.

They are peopled with odd characters oddly unlike you and me in so many ways. Except that in the most important traits, in the most important ways, they are amazingly like the people you and I meet at the store, bump into in our businesses, and live with every day.

They point to amazing worlds filled with extraordinary creatures and characters of a sort we'd never see here. Unless, of course, we opened our eyes and looked.

Ah, what wouldn't I give to be able to paint such pictures with words and create such worlds as J. R. R. Tolkien's Middle Earth and C. S. Lewis' Narnia?![1] Just to have been transported for a little while to such worlds through the written word and to experience their winsome beauty and, wonder of wonders, to learn what those worlds would teach us about ours, is a fine blessing.

Once you've been there, you see, you'd give your last dollar to go there again. To really go there. To live for a few days, or a few centuries, with Bilbo and Frodo and Gandalf, with Peter and Lucy and Aslan. To gaze across Middle Earth and see the Misty Mountains. To run with the children through Narnia and take the journey "further up and further in."[2]

Anyone who could catch even a glimpse of such wonder, such beauty, and still hesitate to spare even a dime of his life's savings, were that the cost of the trip to live for just a while in such stories, is not worthy of them.

May I let you in on a secret? One of the deepest entice- ments of Heaven to me is that, well, if Narnia and Middle Earth aren't exactly there, I'm still quite sure that the most beautiful realities to which even they are but dim though beautiful reflec- tions, are. I can hardly wait to take in their beauty! And if old Bilbo really is there, then so much the better.

Fantasies. The best stories of all, I think. And, of all stories, they may be the most fun to share with little people whose imaginations are still very big.

"Daddy, did that story really happen?"

"Well, my dear little one, maybe it didn't really happen, but of all stories, I promise you, this is one of the most true."

And, dear friends, I choose in this chapter to point to some very significant truths by pointing your attention to two fine fantasies. Perhaps this chapter could aptly be called a tale of two fantasies. It is at least two illustrations from two fantasies of the finest sort.

The first is the most fun by far. The second . . . well, the second is powerful, I think, but it's power does not lie in its beauty, for the fragment I'll share with you has precious little of that.

No, neither one really happened. But both do happen. They really do. Wonderfully, the first. Sadly, the second. Every day.

Now, for the first. Let's go to Narnia.

A Dragon's Tale

C. S. Lewis begins his story, "There was a boy called Eustace Clarence Scrubb, and he almost deserved it. His parents called him Eustace Clarence and his schoolmasters called him Scrubb. I can't tell you how his friends spoke to him, for he had none."[3]

To have friends, you see, one must have some talent at being a friend. Eustace was singularly short of that gift.

He was a very disagreeable little lad who lived in England six or seven years after World War II.

Truth be told, Eustace was discourteous,

arrogant,

self-centered,

priggish,

and whiny.

All of which contributed to make him, and everyone around him, decidedly unhappy. But all of that changed abruptly, and most surprisingly, when in the summer he was visited by two of his cousins, Edmund and Lucy Pevensie, who, by the way, had been to the wonderful, magical, mystical land of Narnia. They really had, though Eustace, of course, steadfastly refused to believe it.

Narnia. A beautiful land where animals talk, and giants and unicorns and all sorts of delightful creatures live, and children have wonderful adventures.

On one lazy summer afternoon, Lucy and Edmund are sitting on the edge of her bed looking at a picture of what they realize is without question a Narnian ship riding the waves, complete with a gilded prow carved and formed to look like the head of a dragon. At the very sight of it, they begin to talk about their longing for Narnia—until Eustace, who has been listening behind the door, bursts in and begins to make fun of them.

But not for long.

As the three kids stand in front of the picture, the painted ocean begins to look amazingly wet, the waves begin to really roll, and gusts of wind begin to blow from the painting through their hair. In the space of a few startling moments, all three children suddenly find themselves launched from a bedroom in England straight into a magical sea where they are fished out and rescued by the crew of the Narnian ship. There on the deck of the *Dawn Treader*, they meet Narnian friends from previous adventures—most notably, Caspian the boy king of Narnia.

Edmund and Lucy are delighted. Eustace is, well, not so thrilled. He makes repeated entreaties that he be taken to the British consul and returned home immediately, and he begins to make of himself an incredible nuisance.

The children have joined Caspian and the *Dawn Treader* as they are sailing east looking for seven lost lords of Narnia. After an interesting adventure or two (which alters Eustace's mood not at all), the ship's company is driven before a terrible storm for days and finally makes land at an uncharted but beautiful island.

As soon as the landing party arrives on shore, Eustace sneaks off by himself to explore the island and, largely, to avoid the work the others are undertaking to refit their ship and replenish their stores.

Eustace hikes into the hills and blunders into a little valley with a pool of water in the middle, a cliff on one side, and a cave near the bottom. As he explores, he is frightened by something large coming out of the mouth of the cave. He hides and watches as a dragon, a very sick dragon, crawls out of the cave, makes its way haltingly toward the edge of the pool, collapses there, and dies.

About that time, rain begins to fall in huge drops. Drenched to the skin, Eustace runs to seek shelter in the cave where, to his amazement, he finds the dead dragon's vast treasure.

The very surprised boy is almost buried by coins and rings, bracelets and diamonds. He greedily begins filling his pockets with everything he can carry, but he is frightened away from the rest of the treasure when he catches a glimpse of what he takes to be the leg of yet another dragon. He dashes out of the cave, runs down to the pool, peers in, sees the other dragon again, and, after a few terrible moments, realizes, in a far more terrible moment, that the "other dragon" whose reflection he sees in the water is himself.

Eustace Scrubb now has the skin to fit his disposition. Through greed and carnality, magic and mystery, some power in the cave, the treasure, the pool, or the valley, he has become a green, scaly, smoke-breathing dragon.

C. S. Lewis unfolds the story far better than I ever could, but, to shorten the tale, I'll simply tell you that Eustace finally managed to rejoin the others, although identifying himself to his shipmates was no easy task. Sailors, on the whole, have never been keen on meeting dragons, and to have a mute dragon of a beast circle their ship and land in the vicinity was disconcerting, to say the least.

They'd been concerned about dragons ever since they had earlier sent out a search party to try to find Eustace and, looking down into a valley, had seen from a distance a dead dragon. The ship's first mate surmised that the beast had eaten Eustace and been poisoned by him, but, in any case, they'd found no sign of their disagreeable shipmate. Then the live dragon had shown up and finally had made them realize the horrible truth that he, the dragon, was Eustace Clarence Scrubb.

Eustace Scrubb. One-time disagreeable boy. Now, newly-dragoned dragon. And there we'll leave him for a little while.

When the Apostle Paul writes to the Ephesians and urges them to maintain the unity of the Spirit and to go on growing in maturity in Christ, he insists that they must no longer have any part in living a life characterized by deeds of darkness—the kind of dark and futile, ignorant and hardened, sensual and impure lifestyle so characteristic of the Gentiles of Paul's day and, of course, so many people in ours. At first glance, it seems strange that Paul, writing to Gentiles, would warn them that they "must no longer live as the Gentiles do."

Paul, have you forgotten your audience?

No. Paul lived in a world harshly divided between Jew and Gentile. But he preached a Lord whose cross broke down that wall of division and distinction. Are his readers, primarily, Gentiles? Yes, but they are more than that. Now they are Christians, "little Christs." Not Gentiles who happen to be Christians, but Christians who happen to be Gentiles and who stand justified before God and in a new relationship to him because of the blood of Christ which freely cleanses believing men and women from all races, colors, and nations. In their redeemed lives and their new walk with Christ there is no room for these Gentiles, or any other Christians, to live "as the Gentiles do." Now, you see, they are Christ's.

The apostle paints a very dark picture of the kind of dark lifestyle that issues from living completely apart from God.

Those who live such lives are "darkened in their understanding," wandering, stumbling, staggering blindly through a miserable existence bereft of light.

They are "separated from the life of God," deathbound and dying, chained to the corpse of their own carnality.

A Dragon's Tale

They are "hardened" in their hearts, consciences calcified, locked into lifeless *rigor mortis*.

In his paraphrase, Eugene Peterson portrays them as "the crowd, the empty-headed, mindless crowd" who have refused "for so long to deal with God that they've lost touch not only with God but with reality itself."4 No wonder they wander.

Directionless.

Dazed.

Despairing.

But their situation is worse even than that. Not only are they lost in every sense of the term, they are given over to, sold out to, madly enslaved to every kind of impure obsession and perversion. They're rushing toward and wildly embracing the destiny of the wolf portrayed in a rather gruesome tale told by Paul Harvey and retold in *Leadership Journal*. How, Paul Harvey asks, does an Eskimo kill a wolf?

> First, the Eskimo coats his knife blade with animal blood and allows it to freeze. Then he adds another layer of blood, and another, until the blade is completely concealed by frozen blood.
>
> Next, the hunter fixes his knife in the ground with the blade up. When a wolf follows his sensitive nose to the source of the scent and discovers the bait, he licks it, tasting the fresh frozen blood. He begins to lick faster, more and more vigorously, lapping the blade until the keen edge is bare.
>
> Feverishly now, harder and harder the wolf licks the blade in the arctic night. So great becomes his craving for blood that the wolf does not notice the razor-sharp sting of the naked blade on his own tongue, nor does he recognize the instant at which his insatiable thirst is being satisfied by his own warm blood. His carnivorous appetite just craves more—until the dawn finds him dead in the snow!5

Not a pretty picture. But a true one. One well-illustrated, I think, by a second flight to fantasy.

How to Measure a Rainbow

The Chronicles of Thomas Covenant the Unbeliever by Stephen R. Donaldson (actually two trilogies, six books) comprise, I think, one of the most amazing fantasy series of our time.[6] I know next to nothing about the author, but I know that his command of the English language and his flair with the pen hold me spellbound as he deftly performs the daunting task of the fantasy spinner. He weaves a world.

The Covenant Chronicles center around the experiences of an intriguing and tragic figure named Thomas Covenant. As the epic fantasy begins to unfold we see Covenant walking woodenly from Haven Farm, his property on the outskirts of a small New England town, into the little hamlet to pay his phone bill. Not so long ago, though it seemed to him a life-time ago, he was a best-selling novelist with a proud and capable wife, a new baby son, and a second book already in progress.

But that had been while he was alive. Now, for all practical purposes, he was dead, though he still breathed and walked and, occasionally, spoke.

He'd been too busy to worry much when a numb purple spot appeared near the base of the little finger of his right hand. Even when the wound which grew in the center of that spot began to spread a bit, he'd had little time to be much concerned. Because he was so intent on his work, and because the wound did not hurt—the numbness permitted no pain—it was becoming seriously infected by the time his wife discovered it and insisted that he allow her to take him to the hospital for treatment. Doctors there quickly diagnosed gangrene, scheduled him for surgery, and ended up removing the smaller two fingers of his right hand.

A Dragon's Tale

And then they pronounced the ugly word which was both his new diagnosis and his lifelong sentence.

Leprosy.

Leprosy, or Hansen's Disease, named for the Norwegian physician Gerard Henrik Armauer Hansen who identified the leprosy bacillus in 1874, is a "chronic, infectious disease that primarily affects the skin, mucous membranes, and nerves." The disease probably started in the Indus Valley in India and spread to the Mediterranean and North African regions until all of Europe became affected.[7]

Most folks in developed nations probably know about the disease largely because of the biblical restrictions regarding lepers and the accounts of Jesus' healing of these sad souls. We know that they were forced to live outside the camp away from their families and society in general, forced to cry "Unclean!" whenever they came near an uninfected person. And we know something of the work of Mother Teresa with the poorest of the poor in India, with outcasts, and with lepers who are part of that pitiable group.

Not as common as it once was, probably five percent of the world population now live in areas and in conditions where they are susceptible to the disease which is found most often in destitute nations where nutrition is very poor indeed. In the whole world, probably 1.15 million people suffer from the disease. 210,000 cases are confirmed in the western hemisphere. In the United States, we have about 640 known cases, with about 160 new cases each year.[8] Most of them are found in immigrants or people who were exposed to the disease in tropical regions as children.[9]

Your chances of winning a state lottery (probably even if you never play) are far better than your chances of contracting leprosy. It is considered to be "perhaps the least infectious of all contagious diseases." The disease's progress can usually be arrested with drug therapy which is readily available in the western world, but at present no cure is available for leprosy, though scientists are working on a vaccine.[10]

One of the worst terrors of this frightening disease, and perhaps the main reason our minds are filled with macabre images of maimed and disfigured wretches consigned to leper colonies, is the fact that leprosy attacks the nerves of its victims and robs them of the ability to feel. With no feeling in their fingers and toes, hands and feet, they can easily injure themselves, often seriously, and never feel pain's warning. Consequently, modern lepers are taught that one of their primary defenses against the ravages of the disease is a strict regimen known as VSE, Visual Surveillance of Extremities, in which they periodically take stock visually of their extremities to be wary of any real or potential injury.[11]

Dr. Paul Brand, a leading authority on Hansen's Disease and, most particularly, reconstructive surgery of the hand, tells with his coauthor Philip Yancey the poignant story of a man from South India named Sadagopan or, more familiarly, Sadan.[12]

Sadan, a well-educated man from a family of high caste, had become an outcast once he became afflicted with leprosy. He was in terrible shape when he came to the leprosy clinic at Vellore. His fingers were already paralyzed and shortened, and his feet were ulcerated and half the length they should have been. But after four years of reconstructive surgeries and relentless work in perfecting special shoes that would not reinjure his feet, Sadan was ready to go home for a weekend visit.

Filled with excitement, Sadan looked forward to the happy reunion with his family. But Dr. Brand was careful to review with him the dangers he faced. You see, he still had no feeling in his hands and feet. Nerves do not regenerate.

The reunion was a joyous one, and on the evening of his

first day at home, Sadan slept in his own room for the first time in four years. But the next morning when he looked at his left hand he recoiled in horror. Part of his index finger was mangled and bleeding. It had been gnawed by a rat, and he hadn't known it. Crushed and disheartened, he was nevertheless more determined than ever to stay the weekend.

The next evening Sadan stood sentry over his own body, reading while his family slept. But late in the night his eyelids betrayed him and he dozed. What he did not know until morning was that his right hand had slid over onto the side of a hot oil lamp. The skin had burned off to the tendons, and he hadn't felt a thing.

For Sadan, the absence of pain was a terrible thing.

Thomas Covenant, the leper in Stephen Donaldson's epic fantasy, is separated from Sadan by oceans and cultures but united with him in the numb isolation and loneliness wrought by leprosy.

Covenant wakes up from his surgery having lost not only half his hand but losing his wife. She stands in a corner of his room, as far away from him as possible, screaming her horror through tears as she hurls prophecies of dire prognoses: You're a leper! Your fingers and toes will rot away! Your arms and legs and facial features will knot and twist! You'll become incapable of feeling! And, if that isn't bad enough, it's a contagious disease and children are among the most susceptible. Most people are infected as children. You'll infect your own son![13]

And so she leaves and takes their son.

And Thomas Covenant is plunged further into a paroxysm of loss. His fingers. His family. His feeling. But his downward spiral is begun by an agony of feeling as he senses his whole world being destroyed.

Even his neighbors shun him. His groceries are delivered, left on the porch. Someone pays his phone bill anonymously, lest Covenant be so bold as to walk into town to pay it himself. Fear reigns in his community, and he becomes a reproach and a curse word to everyone who once might have claimed him as their town's famous novelist. Now he's a leper. An outcast. Unclean.

When Covenant discovers that his fellow citizens are so afraid of him that they're paying his bills lest they have to venture anywhere near him, he rages against the unfairness of it all and walks haltingly to town. In emotional agony, he steps out into a crosswalk, falls in front of a speeding police car, and . . . is transported to another world.

In that world known simply as the Land, the beautiful, life-giving Land and its winsome inhabitants are in peril to an evil figure, Lord Foul. But they cling to old stories of a hero, Berek Halfhand, a legendary half-handed one-time savior of the land who fought powerfully against Foul's evil. They believe Covenant to be his successor. Because he is armed with the precious, magical white gold (unheard of in that land) of his wedding ring, they look to him to save their world, their Land.

But Covenant is "the Unbeliever." He doesn't believe that the Land really exists. It must be a delusion, a dream. All the more so because it is so breathtakingly beautiful and filled with life. It beguiles him with renewed, reclaimed health and feeling.

He rages against it. He can't afford to feel, can't afford to lose the leper's wariness, the constant self-awareness and guard, which keeps him alive in his world, the "real" world to which he knows he must one day return. He remembers just how dangerous a leper's illusion of health, and subsequent loss of self-awareness, can be. Covenant had spent months in a leprosy hospital learning how to deal with the disease everyone called "his" but which held him firmly in its grim grip. He remembers a pitiful inmate of the leprosarium who had failed in his vigilance, who had forgotten that he could not feel.

A Dragon's Tale

To impress upon Covenant the severity of his situation, a doctor at the leprosarium had taken him to this patient's room. As Covenant stepped into the room, he was greeted with the pungent, terrible smell of rotting flesh. A sad and grotesque man, shrunken by the disease, sat on the bed.

Slowly, the patient raised his hands as if to embrace Covenant.

His hands were swollen stumps, fingerless lumps of pink, sick meat marked by cracks and ulcerations from which a yellow exudation oozed through the medication. They hung on thin, hooped arms like awkward sticks. And even though his legs were covered by his hospital pajamas, they looked like gnarled wood. Half of one foot was gone, gnawed away, and in the place of the other was nothing but an unhealable wound.

Then the patient moved his lips to speak, and Covenant looked up at his face. His dull, cataractal eyes sat in his face as if they were the center of an eruption. The skin of his cheeks was as white-pink as an albino's; it bulged and poured away from his eyes in waves, runnulets, as if it had been heated to the melting point; and these waves were edged with thick tubercular nodules.

"Kill yourself," he rasped terribly. "Better than this."

Covenant broke away from the doctor. He rushed out into the hall and the contents of his stomach spattered over the clean walls and floor like a stain of outrage.

In that way, he decided to survive.[14]

The absence of feeling, even of pain, can be a terrible thing, perhaps even a sentence of death or a lifelong chain to something worse.

Actually, the pitiful man at the leprosarium was ruined not just because he could not feel but because he failed to remind himself that he could not feel. Thomas Covenant survives by reminding himself constantly that he cannot feel, cannot afford the illusion of feeling. But in the process, he closes himself off to all human and emotional feeling as well and becomes an unwitting partner of the former wife and the townspeople who look at him as less than human. A leper. An outcast. Unclean. Unfeeling.

Thomas Covenant is a man caught on the horns of a dilemma. To save the Land, to be saved himself, he must open himself to feeling. For a leper in our world, that is impossible. For a leper in the Land who must one day leave behind Land-brought health and feeling and return to our world and to his own numbness, it is dangerous. Thus Donaldson weaves the fantasy which I found hauntingly fascinating.

I share the tale with you, well, partly because I just finished the series and wanted to discuss it with a friend (thanks for listening!) but largely because of this: When I think of Donaldson's portrayal of the pathetic man in the leprosarium, I am reminded of the Apostle Paul's depiction of those who have cut themselves off from God. He describes them as those who have "lost all sensitivity." Regarding that which is right and good and beautiful, they have no feeling.

And that is a very frightening thing.

For lepers.

And for men and women who face the choice of either opening themselves more each day to the life and health and beauty of God or closing themselves off and losing the ability to feel. To really feel. And to recognize the One who gives life.

We left Eustace Scrubb earlier, the sharp-tongued little boy turned fire-breathing dragon.

On the whole, Eustace was actually a much nicer dragon than he had been a little boy. He began to see things in a different light. What was once important to him now seemed much less so. He began to see the greed and selfishness of his former existence. And, in dragon form, he began to do all that he could to help his former shipmates.

He became an accomplished aerial hunter for food.

On cold nights he allowed his friends to sit against his hot sides.

He lit their campfires with his breath.

He let them fly as passengers on his back.

One night, about six days after they'd landed on the island, and after about six days of dragonhood, Eustace the dragon was lying awake, wondering how his strange story would end, when suddenly he was approached by a beautiful and enormous lion. Eustace didn't know it at the time, but the lion's name was Aslan.

Aslan led Eustace up to the top of a mountain he'd never seen before to a lush garden filled with trees and fruit. In the middle of the garden was a crystal clear pond fed by a well. Water bubbled up from the bottom. Marble steps led down into the water.

Eustace began to make his way into the pond, but the lion told him, without actually using words, that first he must undress.

Undress? I don't know how familiar you are with dragons, but I'm sure you'll not be surprised to learn that dragons don't wear clothes. Perplexed at first, Eustace realized that dragons, creatures of a snaky sort, can probably shed their skins. That, he reasoned, must be what the lion meant.

So Eustace began to scratch and peel and tear off his rough, wrinkled, scaly skin. Only scales fell off at first, but then, with great relief and a very pleasant feeling, the whole skin began to be shed. It came off wonderfully and lay "knobbly" and dry on the ground beside him.

He started to step into the pool. Then he looked down and

noticed that his new skin had already become as hard and rough and scaly as the first. He tore it off again, just as he had done before.

Three times he went through the same process, but always underneath was another skin just as dragonish as the one before. The old skins lay on the ground beside Eustace, and he was wondering how many he'd have to take off, when Aslan spoke again. Again, wordlessly.

"You will have to let me undress you."

Eustace was afraid of the lion's claws, but he realized desperately that this, as frightening a process as it might be, was the only way. He lay down flat on his back. And the lion began. Lewis describes it this way:

> "The very first tear he made was so deep that I thought it had gone right into my heart. And when he began pulling the skin off, it hurt worse than anything I've ever felt. The only thing that made me able to bear it was just the pleasure of feeling the stuff peel off. . . .
>
> "Well, he peeled the beastly stuff right off—just as I thought I'd done it myself the other three times, only they hadn't hurt—and there it was lying on the grass: only ever so much thicker, and darker, and more knobbly looking than the others had been. And there was I as smooth and soft as a peeled switch and smaller than I had been. Then he caught hold of me—I didn't like that much for I was very tender underneath now that I'd no skin on—and threw me into the water. It smarted like anything but only for a moment. After that it became perfectly delicious and as soon as I started swimming and splashing I found that all the pain had gone. . . . I'd turned into a boy again.[15]

Eustace was "un-dragoned." Aslan dressed him in new clothes and took him back to the others. From then on, he began to be a very different, and very much improved, little boy.

A Dragon's Tale

When God created humankind in his image with a will that is free, he gave us a wonderful but awesome blessing. We can choose to live by the power of his life, whole and sensitive to his blessing. Or we can choose to be leprous and unfeeling.

We can choose to be dragons, complete with scaly dispositions, sharp teeth that cut and bite, and throats that breathe fire. Or we can choose to submit to Christ and to allow him to release us from that kind of life. To set us free.

Paul says that we can choose "to be made new in the attitude" of our minds. He says that we can "put on the new self, created to be like God in true righteousness and holiness" (4:23-24).

But first we have to shed our "old self." And we can't even do that alone. No self-help plan of improvement will ever cut through deeply enough. Do-it-yourself righteousness is really no righteousness at all. Like Eustace, if we really want to be "undragoned" and whole, we'll have to trust the Lion of the tribe of Judah to undress us by the pardoning power of his sacrifice and to reclothe us in his righteousness by the depth of his transforming love.

Then dragons become Sons and Daughters of God.

Then lepers, outcast and unclean, become clean as the purest and whitest snow.

And our lives are both blessed and a blessing in the very best and truest story of all, the story of God's love.

Chapter 9

Therefore each of you must put off falsehood and speak truthfully to his neighbor, for we are all members of one body. "In your anger do not sin": Do not let the sun go down while you are still angry, and do not give the devil a foothold. He who has been stealing must steal no longer, but must work, doing something useful with his own hands, that he may have something to share with those in need.

Do not let any unwholesome talk come out of your mouths, but only what is helpful for building others up according to their needs, that it may benefit those who listen. And do not grieve the Holy Spirit of God, with whom you were sealed for the day of redemption. Get rid of all bitterness, rage and anger, brawling and slander, along with every form of malice. Be kind and compassionate to one another, forgiving each other, just as in Christ God forgave you. Be imitators of God, therefore, as dearly loved children and live a life of love, just as Christ loved us and gave himself up for us as a fragrant offering and sacrifice to God.

Ephesians 4:25-5:2

Living a Life
of Love

*Be imitators of God, therefore,
as dearly loved children and live a life of love,
just as Christ loved us. . . .*
EPHESIANS 5:1-2

Y ou can't live off of love." We've all heard the warning, and there certainly is truth in the statement that those on the receiving end of this bit of advice would do well to take into account.

But, apparently, there are exceptions to the rule.

Richard Bailey, for example, has quite literally lived off of love very well and very successfully now for a number of years. Here's how he did it.

Stable owner Bailey evidently tired of making money the old-fashioned way, by earning it. According to the indictment against him as reported in *Newsweek*, Bailey allegedly made a fortune by selling nags passed off as fine racing horses to at least thirteen wealthy women in the Chicago area.[1]

Bailey would place a "lonely heart" ad such as this in a suburban paper: *"Attractive, successful professional, SWDM, 53, wavy hair, 5'11", 170 lbs., with a great sense of humor, creative, secure, family-oriented, loves dancing, exercising, long walks, nature, and fine dining. Seeking S/DWF to share happiness & commitment."* And his box number followed.

If that ad sounds "too good to be true," that's because it was.

But more than a few lonely ladies in the Chicago area were

looking for love as they looked in their papers. The hook was baited, and it didn't take long before Bailey began to feel tugs on the line.

What he did not say in the ad was, "Only rich widows and wealthy divorcées need respond," but gals of that description were most certainly the only kinds he was interested in.

When ladies with the proper bank balances made contact with Bailey, he would romance his way into their trust and affection, and set the hook ever deeper. He would wine them and dine them, smooze them and woo them, and then he'd just mention that he happened to know how they could get an absolutely amazing racehorse at a bargain price. What they ended up buying were worthless racehorses at very inflated prices.

The scam worked time and time again. Bailey was good at it. Like the serial killers who are so dangerous precisely because they are so intelligent that they hone and refine their twisted methods each time they strike, this forked-tongued snake slithered his way into the affection—and the pocketbooks—of an ever-increasing list of lonely, gullible, affection-starved but wealthy women.

Sometime in the mid-seventies, Bailey, who was used to taking candy from babes, so to speak, met candy heiress Helen Vorhees Brach, the widow of candy tycoon Frank Brach. If you've ever bit into a store-bought chocolate-covered cherry, chances are you've sampled just one of the many candy confections that carry the Brach name.

Helen was a hostess at a country club when Frank Brach met her. In 1951, she became his third wife.

In 1970, Brach died. Helen, once again alone, found comfort in the companionship of her two dogs, Candy and Sugar. When they died, she had them buried in the family plot, and she became very active in supporting animal rights causes—active to the tune of millions of dollars. And then she met a two-legged critter of a different sort, Richard Bailey.

Bailey never talked Brach into marriage, though he tried. But, according to *Newsweek*, he did smooze her out of $300,000 for racehorses that weren't worth $30,000.

In February 1977, after a checkup at the Mayo Clinic, candy heiress Helen Brach disappeared without a trace. In 1984, she was declared dead. The trail leading to her murderer was stone-cold dead itself.

In 1989, federal agents reopened the case and followed a "trail of fraud" leading to Richard Bailey, and in the process found a side-trail leading to 19 very prominent horse trainers, owners, and veterinarians whom they have charged with scamming insurance companies by paying for the "electrocution, burning, and maiming" of 15 horses "from the mid-seventies until 1991." How prominently Richard Bailey fits into this scam remains to be seen.[2]

In the meantime, though there is no law against taking candy from an heiress, there most certainly is a law against murder. Authorities believe that Helen Brach learned about Bailey's con, threatened to turn him in, and was killed for her discovery. Bailey has denied it, but he was charged recently with conspiring to commit murder.

"You can't live off of love."

Maybe not, but Richard Bailey lived off a very twisted sham of love and lies for lots of years. It was like taking candy from an heiress.

It's one thing to try to live off of love. It's quite another to "live a life of love" (5:2). Try the first, and, at least if you try it with larceny in your heart, you'll live a sham that issues in shame. But attempt the second, and your life becomes ennobled by your mission, a warm-hearted life kindled by Heaven's passionate and beneficent flame, a life warming the lives of those around you.

What beautiful warmth! Which brings me to this . . .

Living in the Warmth of Truth

I love candles. Maybe that's because I'm a firebug from way back.

I'll never forget the day many years ago when my little brother and I came to the kitchen table with a *papier-mâché* volcano we'd built atop a piece of flat cardboard. Our science teacher had given us plans for the diminutive volcano, along with the formula, composed of a mixture of saltpeter and sugar, for the lava. Spoon a bit of the lava mixture into the top of the volcano, drop a match down the crater, and, *voilà!*, lava-like material soon bubbled over the top and rolled innocuously down the sides of the "mountain" while the crater puffed a little polite smoke.

Fine. But just a bit boring.

Jim and I discovered pretty quickly that varying the proportions of chemicals in the lava recipe could spice up the whole concoction quite nicely. Our mother watched as we set the volcano on top of the table, spooned in a bit of the mix (and just a tad extra for good measure, using the if-a-little-is-good-a-lot-is-better approach), backed up, and dropped in the match.

The result was, well, very gratifying.

The *papier-mâché* mountain rumbled for a split second, and then, belching gutturally as if from the depths of a microcosmic hell, that miniature Mount St. Helens spewed forth vitriolic flames three feet high. For long moments after the fire flamed out, soot and ash settled from the atmosphere and drifted lazily, peacefully, down to blanket the kitchen table. What an eruption!

My mother was really surprised.

Jim and I continued to work on that formula for the next year or two and conducted all sorts of experiments that gave us a great deal of pleasure.

Our mother was a very patient woman.

I suppose I've always been amazed and fascinated by fire. Our church's fire insurance won't allow volcanoes in my study, but atop my desk sit two candles—one, the lightly-scented three-wick sort, and the other, the heavily-scented, jar-encased variety—and I've found myself today not only enjoying their scent, but occasionally even warming my hands over their flame.

No, this is not an Ebenezer Scrooge/Bob Cratchit situation where a candle and a piece of miserly coal are the only warmth allowed me. My office comes complete with heat.

But it's a really cold day outside. Not exactly a Chamber of Commerce day. I can hear the wind howling. And, worse, the dust has started blowing. I like seasons, and winter is one of my favorite. But today seems to be an unpleasant amalgamation of the least winsome aspects of both winter and spring. I don't know anybody who likes cold wind mixed with dust.

In the midst of a cold and somewhat dreary day, the warm glow of the candles on my desk is a comfort and a blessing. Little sparks of captured sun-fire, beneficent light-wraiths radiating heartwarming light and heat, they seem to chase away the chill and bleakness which might otherwise eclipse the day. Compared to the raw power of a Mount St. Helens, or even the flash-flame of a souped up tabletop volcano, these little lights are small. But even their tiny flickering flames carry warmth and light invested by the God of all warmth, all light, with real power.

How to Measure a Rainbow

In a cold world, a world often chilled by deception and frosted over by falsehood, God's people are to shine like lights as they radiate the warmth of his love and truth.

Have you ever been drafted into unloading a clothes dryer full of bedsheets and comforters, lugged the still-warm load to the bed, and then, feeling their wonderful warmth, just wrapped up in them and collapsed on the bed to let your pores drink in the evanescent but delicious warmth before it faded away?

Have you ever slept a little late on a Saturday morning, carried a heart-warming book to a couch near an east-facing picture window, stretched out, and just basked in the warmth of the sunlight streaming through the window sun-kissing and caressing, enfolding and invigorating your skin—and your spirit?

Have you walked down a beautiful beach and felt the warmth of the sun pouring over you like liquid luminescence cascading in luxurious waves from Heaven to earth?

The life-affirming warmth of truth living in the lives of God's people is like that. Falsehood is cold soil in which nothing much, and certainly nothing good, can grow.

Keith Miller is on target when we says, "I am convinced that although honesty may not be the front doorway to the kingdom of God, it is the *latchstring* to every doorway in His house."[3] Lots of doors slam shut without it, banged to by the force of falsehood.

To be given over to lying is to die a little with each lie.

Honesty is healing.

And honesty begins in the mirror.

Isn't it odd how hard it is at times to be honest with ourselves? When we begin to lie to ourselves, we're well on our way down a path which leads to lying to others, and, ultimately, hiding even from God.

Lies easily become cancers eating away at our souls.

Healing comes only when we expose our lies to the

cleansing warmth of God's truth and deal with falsehood as the life-destroying malignancy that it is.

But that is not easy.

The Lies We Tell Ourselves

The irony is that many people who are in the midst of deluding themselves most seriously do so because they are really too honest to be comfortable while pursuing their present destructive course without first lying to themselves about its consequences.

Listen to the lies we tell ourselves.

"I know Bob doesn't seem to care about his relationship with God now, but once we're married, he'll change and become the spiritual leader of our home."

"Yes, of course, drunkenness is a bad thing, but I really don't have an alcohol problem. I can quit drinking whenever I choose. I just don't think that now is a good time."

"Yes, I know that by pushing for this divorce to chase after the lover who is not my spouse, I am breaking every vow I once held dear, but I have very good reasons, you see, and I can do it without any permanent damage to myself or my kids. I need this divorce to be happy."

"If I just work a little harder, a little longer, make a little more money, finish one more big project, then I'll take time to slow down and spend time with my family, but until then, little pieces of 'quality time' are good enough."

And maybe the most dangerous lie of all: "I'm too strong, too good, too committed to Christ, to ever tell myself the lies listed above or any of the million and one others just like them. Lots of people make those mistakes, but I never would."

Feel the cold, fell draft blowing off of falsehood. Stand in that wind long enough, and it'll freeze your very soul. The cold will hurt at first. But soon you'll be numbed by falsehood's chill. When death comes, you may not feel a thing.

When God came on the scene back in Genesis 3 and found Father Adam and Mother Eve with forbidden fruit juice still trickling down the corners of their mouths, the Bible says that just before they stood lying to their God they suddenly realized that they were naked, and they were ashamed.

Strange. The only way we their children can be
>healed
>>and whole
>>and unashamed

is to stand naked before God once again, laying aside the shabby rags of our self-deception, opening ourselves to be clothed in the pure white robes of his truth,

>>his warmth,
>>>his light,
>>>his Son.

Truth is life. Real. And powerful. And abiding.

The light of truth eclipses and effaces falsehood as we honestly open our hearts and our lives to the One in whom there is no darkness or duplicity at all, and we confess the vast wretchedness of our sin and the mortal depth of our need.

Just to be honest before him.

It maybe the hardest thing we've ever done, but he'll help us do it—if we'll just ask. That's all he's waiting for. He'll walk with us. And he'll wrap us up in the warmth of his embrace.

Oh, you should try wrapping up in a dryer-warmed comforter. No kidding, it's a good thing. But the warmth of *the* Comforter, the Spirit of the living God, is an infinitely better thing.

How do God's people live warmly in a cold world?

With the flame of his Spirit kindled in their hearts.

With the warmth of his love enfolding every aspect of their lives.

Living a Life of Love

With the very power that raised Christ to new life—far more powerful even than the fiery eruption of a Mount St. Helens—wonderfully erupting in their reborn, redeemed, and ransomed lives.

But if you want that warmth in your heart and that power in your life, you must ask God's help in guarding against the chilly wind that would blow out the flame and snuff out its comfort.

No wonder the apostle warns us about going to bed in the icy grip of anger.

Or sneaking around coldheartedly to take what is not ours instead of realizing that we already have a lot, and that everything we have is a God-given gift given to be shared.

Or using our tongues in ways that point to frost in our souls.

Or freezing out the flame of God's Spirit by clinging to the icy bitterness of cold, hard, malicious and unforgiving hearts.

God loves us. He'll lead us, he'll guide us, he'll enliven us with the warmth of his pure flame in our souls. But we must say yes to his kindling.

Do you want to be God's and live life warmly? Do you want to say yes to the warm life and power of his Spirit? The apostle tells us how:

> Watch what God does, and then you do it, like children who learn proper behavior from their parents. Mostly what God does is love you. Keep company with him and learn a life of love. Observe how Christ loved us. His love was not cautious but extravagant. He didn't love in order to get something from us but to give everything of himself to us. Love like that.[4]

The Extravagance of God's Love

Do you realize how much, how well, how deeply God has loved us?

Look at his Son.

Gaze with wonder at the extravagance of his love.

Marvel at the strength and the significance, the purity and the power, of that heart-warming, health-bringing, soul-healing flame.

The God who gives us life gave his Son. When the Babe of Bethlehem drew his first breath of air in the world he had spun into existence eons ago, he became Immanuel, God with us, God in the flesh, God who came into this world laying aside the robes of royalty, God willingly clothed in the garment of humanity, to fully experience our joys and our sorrows, our triumphs and our tears.

I love John Drescher's story of the little boy who lies awake terrified by a storm late one night. From his dark shadowy room he cries out to his father, "Daddy, come, I'm scared." His father, not anxious to leave his own warm bed, tries to console him from afar.

"Oh, son, God loves you and he'll take care of you."

But the little boy, still trembling, shouts back, "I know God loves me and he'll take care of me, but right now I need somebody with skin on!"[5]

Our world did, too. God loved us so much that he came into this world sharing fully in the human situation from the trauma of birth to the violence of death, feeling everything a human being can feel.

God is no absentee landlord living a million miles away leaving the poor tenants lost and alone while a sin-infested world rots and falls down around them.

God is not an emotionless lawgiver, a heavenly bureaucrat lost somewhere on a cloud shuffling paper and handing down rules to complicate a situation he knows nothing about.

God is not the sort of military officer who proposes brave and daring offensives but whose idea of leading the charge is sitting safe and warm in a command post moving markers and flags on a map.

Living a Life of Love

God has lived in this world. He knows how it works and how we can best live. Our God has been to the Front and seen the blood.

The most precious of all was his.

Ah, the extravagance of such love! But what else would you expect from the Artist who splashes the canvas of this world with color in a million hues when black and white and shades of gray probably would have done? No miser, this Creator.

He's the God who not only gives us life, he gives us joy.

He's the God who not only gives us a new day, he gives us new hope each day.

He's the God who not only sends his Son to die for us, he transfuses his Spirit into our hearts so that we can truly live.

When everything else in this world falls, God's love stands.

When our false foundations crumble, God's love endures.

When Satan's winter chills, God's love warms.

Stronger than death.

Longer-lasting than suffering.

Deeper than any temptation to despair.

To live a life of love is to share with those around us the strong, enduring, deep love of the God who has loved us, warmed us, enlivened us, through his own Son. And so . . .

Loved
Warmed
Healed
Loved
Bask in the gracelight from Heaven above
And know that God the Father, the Son, the Dove
Uttered your name before a vast eternity,
And be
Warmed
Healed
Loved.6

"You can't live off of love," the saying goes.

Maybe you can.

Con artist Richard Bailey tried to in a very twisted sort of way. I'd certainly not recommend that.

But God assures us that the very best way to live is to live out of a heart of love.

You can't believe Richard Bailey. You'd best not buy a used car—or a horse—from that sort of crawling creep.

But you can believe the God who loved you so much that he sent his Son to live in this world—out of love. It's because of him that I tell you the good news right now: You *can* live off of love if it's the love of God.

The love of God expressed through his only Son.

The love of God emblazoned before the whole universe.

The love of God lifted up and displayed for all to see atop a wooden cross and a hill called Calvary.

Because of that love, now we, his "dearly loved children," are pardoned and empowered to be "imitators of God" and to "live a life of love, just as Christ loved us" (5:1-2).

Chapter 10

But among you there must not be even a hint of sexual immorality, or of any kind of impurity, or of greed, because these are improper for God's holy people. Nor should there be obscenity, foolish talk or coarse joking, which are out of place, but rather thanksgiving. For of this you can be sure: No immoral, impure or greedy person—such a man is an idolater—has any inheritance in the kingdom of Christ and of God. Let no one deceive you with empty words, for because of such things God's wrath comes on those who are disobedient.
Therefore do not be partners with them.
For you were once darkness, but now you are light in the Lord. Live as children of light (for the fruit of the light consists in all goodness, righteousness and truth) and find out what pleases the Lord. Have nothing to do with the fruitless deeds of darkness, but rather expose them. For it is shameful even to mention what the disobedient do in secret. But everything exposed by the light becomes visible, for it is light that makes everything visible. This is why it is said:

"Wake up, O sleeper,
rise from the dead,
and Christ will shine on you."

Ephesians 5:3-14

To Live in the Light

For you were once darkness,
but now you are light in the Lord.
Live as children of light. . . .
EPHESIANS 5:8

H ave you ever been afraid of the dark? Most of us have. Most of us can probably remember crawling into bed as children—and maybe older children than we'd care to admit—peering out from under the covers into the darkness of our bedroom, and then cringing a bit as our light-starved eyes gazed into the big, dark, open closet on the other side of the room and our minds began to dredge up all sorts of sinister spectres lurking inside. If you've never gotten up out of bed for the express purpose of shutting those closet doors and thus curtaining off that bit of darkness, you were probably a very unusual child!

"Leave a light on, Daddy!"

What father hasn't heard that?

It's not so much that the kids are frightened of getting up in the night and bumping into the furniture.

No.

What they're afraid of is looking out into the darkness and bumping into one of the imaginary night critters that lurks in the dark depths of all of our minds!

I doubt we ever outgrow that fear completely. We seem to have an instinctive dread of the dark that's as much a part of us as our instinct to eat when hungry.

How to Measure a Rainbow

So I suppose we big, mature, courageous adults had just better come clean and admit it—we are still sometimes afraid of the dark!

Are those fears largely irrational? Are they real?

Yes and yes.

If confession is what's called for, I suppose I'd better confess right now myself.

More than a few times I've found myself working in my study at the church fairly late at night, the sun having long since gone down, and I've noticed a couple of things. About me and about the situation.

First of all, I've noticed that I almost always shut the door to the study. It's not always shut during the day. What, pray tell, is the difference? The only difference I can see is that at night that door serves as a kind of wooden dam holding back the deluge of darkness pooled out there in the sanctuary lest it rush in and capsize my little corner coracle of light.

You know what else I've noticed? There is hardly any place more spooky at night than the dark "innards" of a church! And, yes, I know that is completely irrational. Of all the places in my life, the inside of this church is among the warmest and most peaceful, calmest and most beautiful, safest and most serene. In this place, I meet with others I love to share God's love, to meet and commune with him, to reaffirm our vows and renew our commitment, to experience the joy of his presence and our praise in worship.

But that's almost always with the lights on!

If I'm down here at night, I rarely turn on the lights in the foyer. I can navigate just fine in the darkness. But I've noticed that my pace always quickens when I round the corner from the study and turn toward that outside door. It's dark! And there's that big dark expanse right behind me. The lights are off and what was beautiful is now just black. Stand still long enough and the darkness seems to deepen. The sanctuary suddenly seems a bit sinister.

Probably all it would take to throw me into a sudden and almost certainly fatal heart attack would be for me to feel someone quietly place a hand on my shoulder in that dark foyer just as I was about to turn the knob and step out the door! If I didn't die outright, I would create a brand new opening in the side of the building before you could say "scared spitless."

Irrational. I know.

There's nothing to be afraid of. I know. (This is Muleshoe, not Chicago.)

But I also know that this church is still spooky at night, and I've never seen one that wasn't.

And . . . I'd bet my bottom dollar that our kids aren't the only ones who know what it's like to be a bit scared of the dark.

Forever in the Darkness

Have you ever wondered what it would be like to be forced to live in the darkness always? Like you, I'm pretty fond of each of my five senses. I can't imagine wanting to be without any of them, but I imagine most of us would say the one we'd least like to lose would be our sense of sight. To be completely and forever (at least in this life) in the dark would be for most of us a very frightening prospect. We don't like the dark!

One of the things I like best about the Christ we meet in the Gospels is that he was a dispeller of darkness in more ways than one. To heal spiritual blindness is a far greater miracle, I know, but I'm still thrilled when I read about Christ bringing light back into the eyes of the physically blind. What a great gift! How exciting to be able to open blind eyes and offer light and hope and joy!

How to Measure a Rainbow

I think, for example, of the man we meet in John 9, a man who we're told was born blind. He'd never seen a sunset, never seen the faces of his loved ones. Color was to him a meaningless concept. You might as well try to explain "dry" to a fish. He'd lived in darkness. Darkness was all he understood. Until he met Jesus.

It was on this occasion, just before he restored the sight of this man born blind, that Jesus declared, "I am the light of the world" (John 9:5).

Then Jesus made a dirt-and-saliva mud mixture and daubed it on the man's eyes. He sent him to wash in a rock-cut pool called the Pool of Siloam, a part of the amazing water system developed by the great King Hezekiah.

A blind man shuffles to the pool.

A blind man bends to dip his hands into the water.

A blind man rinses blind dead eyes.

But a sighted man jumps to his feet with shouts of joy and eyes now alive, wide open, and twinkling with laughter.

As Siloam sparkles with light, eyes washed first with Siloam's water are now splashed with God's light and color and wave after wave of brand new beauty. God created the world eons before, but for one once-blind man with mud-streaked cheeks and with tears of sheer joy mixing with the new light in his eyes, the world was created anew that day beside the Pool of Siloam.

What a miracle!

Unfortunately, some blindness is still close at hand even on that great day. The blindest men in the whole story are still blind as the proverbial bat. They are the religious leaders who can see only the fact that Jesus performed this miracle on the Sabbath! They see only a broken law, only a shattered rule.

Darkness rears its head again as these blindest of blind men call the newly-sighted man on the carpet. They fuss and fume and filibuster until the man is completely exasperated by their spiritual blindness and their terminal thickheadedness.

"Now that is remarkable!" he says. "You don't know where this Jesus comes from, yet he opened my eyes."

And he proceeds to teach the teachers a lesson.

"We know that God does not listen to sinners. He listens to the godly man who does his will. Nobody has ever heard of opening the eyes of a man born blind. If this man were not from God, he could do nothing" (John 9:30-33).

For his trouble and his speech, they throw him out of the synagogue. But there is no doubt that the blindest men on the scene that day are the pompous Pharisees who claim to see much more clearly than anyone else. Jesus himself tells them, and I'm paraphrasing here, but this is the gist of it, "If you really were blind, you would probably have better sense than you do. At least you would have some excuse for your lack of vision. It's because you claim to see so clearly that you're guilty of sin!"

It was much easier, you see, for Christ to heal the eyes of the man born blind than it was for the One who created light to try to illumine the lives of the self-righteous and the arrogant who claimed to see better than anyone else but who much preferred their darkness to God's light.

Another Confession

How do you react to this story?

For my part, I'm reminded by it that another confession is in order.

It's never very nice to make fun of blind people.

With regard to these blind Pharisees, it's tempting.

But if I fall to that temptation, then I prove how completely blind I am to the fact that I'm often as much in the dark spiritually as they were.

How to Measure a Rainbow

The sight-challenged Pharisees took themselves far too seriously and their God not seriously enough. So sometimes do I.

The nearsighted Pharisees could see only as far as their rules. Their vision blurred before they could make out God's mercy. Color me all too often blind with the very same spiritual myopia.

The Pharisees were blind to their own faults even as they put magnifying glasses over the faults of others. Guess who's done that, too?

Most frightening of all is that the Pharisees were not just passively blind because of immaturity and ignorance. They stood before the Author of Light who could have penned new chapters in their lives, chapters filled with health and vision. But they preferred to scrawl "DARKNESS" over their own hearts, shut their eyes, and close the book on hope. That frightens me because in certain areas of my own life, I may actually prefer darkness to light.

It's genetic, you know.

It's a family thing.

It's been true ever since Eden.

When Father Adam and Mother Eve chose to rebel against God in Eden, to disobey and reject God's good plan by going their own way, they cursed their children by choosing darkness over light. Theirs was not just the choice between eating a particular fruit or not. No, theirs was the choice between living life in God's light by honoring him as Lord or living life in the hell of self-will by choosing to enthrone themselves as the lords of their own lives. It was a defining choice pointing to the very heart of that which is good and that which is evil. And they chose evil.

Do you remember the scene in the movie *Indiana Jones and the Last Crusade* where the adventurers in search of the fabled Holy Grail stand before a whole row of differently-styled chalices, only one of which is the true Grail?[1]

To Live in the Light

As the story goes, to drink from the Holy Grail is to drink immortality, but to drink from a false grail is to drink death. The villain in the movie, completely full of himself, power hungry and greed-crazed, steals the opportunity to choose first. We find out later that the genuine Grail is a very simple hand-fashioned wooden goblet befitting a carpenter from Nazareth. But the bad guy greedily grabs the most richly-ornamented chalice, a golden and jewel-encrusted goblet, dips it into the pool of water, lifts it to his lustful lips, and gulps down a huge drink.

And for a split second, nothing happens. Nothing at all.

But then the winds of immortality thrust horribly into reverse begin to howl, and they blow the man's life away as before our eyes he ages decades and centuries in a few terrible seconds. The rot and decay in his soul become the rot and decay sucking the very life out of him as we watch aghast at the scene unfolding. His putrefied skeleton collapses into a pile of putrescent dust.

And the old Keeper of the Grail who has just witnessed the whole thing intones in the finest piece of dry understatement I've ever heard, "He chose poorly."

When Adam and Eve chose for self and against God, they chose poorly, very poorly indeed (and they chose, I think, in almost exactly the same spirit as the freeze-dried fellow in the movie!).

It was a bad choice then. It is a bad choice now. But it is one we, their children, have continued to make.

My friend, teacher, and mentor Dr. John Victor Halvorson puts it this way: "This age of darkness began with Adam in his rebellion. It has continued over and over again, and my own rebellion has become a part of it."[2]

We are born into a dark world, darkened by the rebellion against the Author of Light. It's as if the rebellion of Adam and Eve was the cataclysmic seismic event that set the terrible tidal wave in motion. Added to that has been the rebellion of each of their children until the tsunami of darkness which has ensued has threatened to destroy us all.

The Dawning of the Light

It was into this dark world that Jesus, the Light of the world, was himself born.

Under a star.

Shining with pure light.

Jesus, God in the flesh, enters this world as the only child ever born of woman who did not share in Adam's sin. Jesus, the Son, the only human being never to choose for the darkness and against the light by rebelling against the Father, draws his first earthly breath at Bethlehem.

The infinite and eternal One lives in this dark timebound world for thirty years and pronounces, with no hint of arrogance, no current of ego, no trace of falsehood, just the deep, quiet strength of truth, "I am the light of the world" (John 8:12). And then one day the hand that flung the stars across the sky wipes mud across the eyes of a blind man. The Starkindler's breath blows life into the cold embers of dead eyes and fans them into glowing and glorious color. Living flame dances its way across the newly-kindled field of a moments-ago-blind man's vision, and Jesus becomes the light of *his* world.[3]

Ah, if we can just open our own eyes for a moment, we'll see that what happened in the life of this blind man is a miracle that can happen in our dark lives as well! This is not, you see, just a wonderful story that happened "once upon a time." It is your story. And mine.

Take just a moment to stop and look into the face of this once-blind man, and you may see a face you recognize. Do you see your own face there? I see mine!

To Live in the Light

You and I were born into a dark world, born blind, born into a race visually-challenged by sin, born into Adam and Eve's family with a darkened nature that will inevitably choose sin by choosing self over God. That man in John 9 is not the only man born blind. Spiritually, all of us are.

But then comes the wonderful day when we meet the Lord, and our darkness meets the Son. Blind, we trust in the Lord for sight. Sin-stained, we wash, but it is his power that cleanses. God through Christ begins to act in our lives to dispel our darkness with his marvelous light.

No one but God could have pierced the darkness of formless chaos with the light of creation.

No one but the God of light can shatter the deep shadows of our sin and act in our lives to take away the darkness.

No one but God can kindle into existence new stars to light the field of our vision.

We who have been born blind come to the Lord of light asking for the gift of sight that can be received in no other way than through faith in the only One who has never participated in, never re-enacted, Adam's sin.

Father Adam was the founder of a race that chose darkness instead of light. Jesus Christ, who the Apostle Paul calls the Second Adam, has become through his death and resurrection the Founder of a race that has chosen to live in the light.

Blind men and women, we cry out for light. And God, the Father of lights in whom "there is no darkness at all," acts (1 John 1:5).

Every time we choose for Christ, we choose for light and against darkness. To reject Christ is to choose to remain in the darkness. It is to choose very poorly. To accept Christ is to choose to open our lives to God's glorious light.

And that's the lesson of John 9 to all of us who know what it is like to be born blind.

How to Measure a Rainbow

If that's all the truth we carry away from these pages, that would be plenty. But I'd like for us to let these thoughts on light and darkness carry us on to some other truths taught by another once-blind man.

Lessons for People Born Blind

It took a literally blinding vision on the road to Damascus to stop a man named Saul, a native of Tarsus, dead in his tracks. In a sort of reverse miracle, God had to blind Saul before the apostle with Paul's vision could be born.

In Ephesians 5, it is an apostle with faith's vision who shares some important lessons for people born blind, people whose only claim to clear vision is their allegiance to the Lord of light.

First of all, the apostle wants us to remember what we were before, and what we would be now, if Christ's light had not come into our lives.

It's pretty obvious, isn't it?

We'd be blind.

Do you realize that the folks Christ picked to be his closest associates were not people distinguished from others by their highly-developed vision? No, they had precious little light of their own to share with a dark world. Still he chose them.

They were inconspicuous nobodies by the world's standards. Peasants. Fishermen. Tax collectors. Rabble-rousers. They were a miserable little crowd.

Only Jesus knew how miserable.

Jesus knew better than they where they would falter and fail, how they would sleep when they should watch, how they would deny when they should confess.

Christ knew that the Twelve themselves would be fussing at the holiest meal they would ever eat with their Lord, and he would be the only one who would stoop to serve.

To Live in the Light

He knew that Peter would whip out a sword to defend him one moment and a tongue to deny him the next.

He knew that they would all scatter like frightened quail when he needed them most.

Apart from their Lord, they were a wretched group of ragtag blind men. In that respect, I'm afraid they looked awfully similar to Christ's modern-day disciples whose claim to vision would be a complete farce if not for the Lord's light.

But the Lord of light and sight and vision looked at them knowing full well who they were and what they would do, and he proclaimed them to be the salt and light of the world.

Just like he does us.

He makes us light. He brings us sight.

Without him, we'd be in darkness. Blind we'd be without his light.

We don't know much about what happened later in the life of the man Jesus healed in John 9, but surely he never forgot that once he had been blind, and that his sight was a gift of grace. Remember what you've come from, and you'll never forget what a precious gift you've been given. To forget your healing is to forget your Healer.

Once "you groped your way through that murk" of darkness, Paul reminds the Ephesians.[4] And when he reminds them, he reminds us. We dare not forget who opened our eyes to the light.

"Live as Children of Light"

But that brings us to Paul's second prescription for people who were born blind but who've been given new sight by the Lord. To each of us, he says, "Live as children of light!"

Once you were in the dark.

Once you were blind, "but no longer. You're out in the

179

open now. The bright light of Christ makes your way plain. So no more stumbling around."[5]

I well remember one bright and beautiful clear day of my childhood, part of which I spent groping around through murky, and in this case, mucky, darkness.

Jim, my two-years-younger brother, and I were off down and around the block, exploring. "Alley-ratting," by which term we meant discovering what neat trash our neighbors were throwing away, just didn't seem exciting enough that day. Chasing tadpoles in the drainage culvert down at one end of the little neighborhood park also somehow seemed a bit too boring. But crawling through a drainage pipe seemed like just the thing to do.

May I hasten to say that it *wasn't* a good thing to do. It was a senseless and stupid and dangerous thing to do. And you really should not try this at home or anywhere else.

But try it we did.

Our family lived in the West Hills subdivision of Amarillo during all of my first eighteen years of childhood. (I am now in my 44th year of childhood.) West Hills implies that we had some. Hills, that is. We did have a few of what in our part of the country (the High Plains of Texas which are flat as a flitter, whatever a flitter is) and in that fair city (Amarillo, that is) pass for hills. Down in the wee valley between them was West Hills Park. And running down through the center of West Hills Park was, at one time, an open concreted drainage ditch conducting water from one end of the park and the neighborhood to the other. The park authorities, though, had wisely decided that part of the park would make a fine playing field for a variety of sports if they covered the open ditch and buried concrete drainage pipe to do invisibly but efficiently the same job the ditch once did.

Fine.

It was a good plan.

To Live in the Light

But the authorities had not planned on two preacher's kids being dumb enough to crawl through their pipe. I don't remember signs at the openings of the pipe saying, "Don't Be Stupid and Crawl Through This Thing." This incident took place in the days before our litigious society was quite so litigious, before the days when juries (evidently even more intellectually-challenged than the dim-witted plaintiffs to whom they grant large settlements) rewarded clumsy people for dumping hot coffee in their own laps, or really foolish people for shoving garden hoses down their throats and turning the faucet on. The story I'll tell you took place in the years before it was quite so easy to find a slime-oozing shyster smiling on the back cover of most cities' phone books. Jim and I had two chances of receiving a large settlement from the City of Amarillo and profiting financially from our stupidity if something went wrong while we were crawling through that pipe: slim and none.

But if Jim was dumb, I was dumber. The plan, you see, was not that we both crawl through the pipe. The plan was that *I* crawl through the pipe. (Jim's idea, probably.) Though it's obvious now that precious little thought entered into this plan at all, we thought we'd thought of everything. We even had walkie-talkies so that the explorer crawling inside the pipe (that would be me) would have backup on the outside in case he got into trouble (that would be Jim).

But what could go wrong?

Oh, *lots* could go wrong. I know that now.

Let's talk about bites, stings, and other potential poisoning. Let's discuss what might happen should the human crawler unwittingly corner a large rodent or other pipe-loving critter inside a really confined space. You might want to mention potential drowning. Asphyxiation would also make for a pretty bad day. An attack of claustrophobia somewhere in the middle of a snaking 100-plus-yard-long pipe might also be a bit unpleasant. But I suppose the resulting sheer terror of any of these unpleasantries would at least be a way to spice up an otherwise boring summer afternoon.

Lots could go wrong.

But I crawled into the pipe.

It was a hands-and-knees proposition from the very first. The pipe was not even nearly large enough for even a child to stand up. Water mingled with and marinated the dirt down at the bottom to produce just enough mud that crawling through the pipe became a hands-and-knees-pressed-sort-of-hard-to-the-sides proposition for a good part of the trip.

One other problem presented itself almost immediately. The walkie-talkies did not work. Or, if they worked at all, they worked very poorly and for just a little while. I've still not tested this scientifically, but walkie-talkies don't seem to like concrete pipe.

But the lack of high-tech communication was not the biggest problem.

No. The biggest problem was the dark.

I was doing pretty well as long as I could see light streaming in from the "entrance." But that pipe snaked around a good bit under that playing field and, one or two turns down the pike (or the pipe), the light played out completely.

I wasn't totally stupid. I did have a flashlight. But the inside of that pipe became about the darkest place I've seen in my entire life. My little flashlight became my lifeline, but it was precious little match for that palpable darkness. I wasn't sure how long the batteries would last. And I was beginning to wonder how the park people could get ten miles of pipe under what on the well-lit and sunny surface seemed to be just a little over 100 yards of field.

Periodically I'd stop to catch my breath. My own breathing was about all I could hear, though some other occasional echoes seemed ominous. I probably didn't know enough to wonder about the levels of sewer gas in a pipe that was not supposed to be a sewer but which I could have turned into one pretty quickly. I probably didn't know the word "claustrophobia" but it was indeed beginning to be a significant problem. I just wanted out, and my "rest" breaks became not times to rest as much as times to turn off my puny little light to see if I could catch just a glimpse of God's light coming through at the other end.

Nothing.

Over and over again. Nothing.

Nothing but darkness.

But I will never forget the feeling of relief and genuine joy flooding over me when I crawled around one more of what seemed like a million curves and saw light beginning to shine from what had to be the other end of that dark pipe.

For a light-starved lad that light was delicious. It was beautiful. It was magnificent. I thrilled to drink in great draughts of the liquid luminescence that came flooding over me. In the middle of a whole city of people going about their everyday tasks and taking light for granted, one little boy gave thanks to God for light that was absolutely on that day Heaven's very best gift to a tired and dumber-than-average human sewer rat crawling out of a pipe in West Hills Park in Amarillo, Texas.

Thank God for light!

The God Who Opens Our Eyes

Multiply my relief on that ancient occasion a thousand times and you may have some dim appreciation for the way the blind man in John 9 must have felt when through the mud he was rinsing off of his face the light began to shine.

God acted in an amazing way in the life of the man born

blind. But he has acted in amazing ways in your life and mine, too!

In Christ, Paul says, you have been called to be "light in the Lord" (5:8). God has acted in your life to make you truly alive. Now, live into that calling!

Once your eyes were blind and closed to the light. The Lord of light opened them! Now, keep them open!

Can you do that? Can I?

No.

We can't.

You can't. I can't.

But Christ can.

Without him, we can't keep the darkness at bay. We who were powerless to heal our own blindness are just as powerless, on our own, to sustain our sight.

But the good news is not only that Christ has opened our eyes; the good news is that the same Lord who gave us sight is the Lord who empowers us to keep it.

Can you imagine Paul's deep love and concern for the Ephesians, his spiritual children?

He'd loved them,

taught them,

nurtured them,

turned their faces toward the light.

He's an older man now, an aged apostle, locked away from the ones he loves so much. But his pen is unconfined. He writes to his loved ones who lived in the shadow of one of the wonders of the ancient world, the great Temple of Artemis (or Diana). He writes to people who have lived right in the middle of the darkness of paganism, separated from the light of Christ, to remind them that the One who called them to *be* light is the One who empowers them to *live* as light.

To Live in the Light

I was a young preacher, just starting out, a still-wet-behind-the-ears proclaimer of the Light, when I was privileged to sit at the feet of a veteran pastor and teacher of God's people, Dr. John Victor Halvorson, the good gentleman I mentioned earlier. He was a gray-haired, Norwegian Lutheran with a deep love for God and God's people. Time and again, I remember Dr. Halvorson reminding his young colleagues in kind Norwegian-tinged tones that in baptism, in the Lord's Supper, in prayer, in the indwelling of Christ's Spirit, it is God who acts in the lives of his people claiming us as his children, the children of light. Through Christ, the Father has acted in our lives to forgive us of all sin, and Dr. Halvorson reminded us in the words, I believe, of a noted theologian (though I'm not enough of a theologian myself to remember who), that Christ's mandate to us is this: "Become now in life what you've been called to be! Become now in actual life what you already are in Christ Jesus!" Dr. Halvorson would always go on to make the eminently biblical point that the demands of God are always rooted in God's mighty acts. When God asks us to do something in our lives, he asks us to do something that is possible only because, but marvelously because, of what he has already done *for* us.[6]

God has called us to be light in a dark world.

God has called us to be light that illuminates and chases away darkness and evil.

God has called us to live our lives redemptively and transparently in the beauty of his light.

God has called us to *be* light.

And we are able to become what he has called us to be because of Christ and what he has already done for us on the cross and what he promises to do for us each day pardoning us through his blood and empowering us through his Spirit.

We who were once blind have been called to be "light in the Lord." Now through Christ we are to live into that calling. We are to "live as children of light" (5:8).

What proceeds from this kind of living, Paul says, is the wonderful fruit which the light of Christ gives power to grow.

Goodness. Righteousness. Truth.

That sort of fruit won't grow in the murk and mire of the darkness. But it will grow marvelously in the light, and we're to live as children of the light, not as creatures crawling around in darkness.

The light of God.

It exposes evil. It brings healing.

Even a little light in a dark room goes a long way toward dispelling darkness. Evil flourishes in darkness, but once exposed for what it is, it begins to lose much of its power.

Interesting, isn't it?, that the worst dives in any community from dreary bars to filthy "adult" bookstores are almost always dens of darkness shuttered off from the light.

Paul warns, "Have nothing to do with the fruitless deeds of darkness, but rather expose them" (5:11). Open the shutters, take off the blinders, and allow God's light first to expose and then to illumine, to cleanse, and to heal.

One commentator describes what happens when Christ's light is allowed to shine:

> Christ, as the center of God's sphere of influence, beams out its light on the darkness of this world, like a spotlight playing on the stage of a darkened theater. Believers stand in the beam and become identified with and live in its light. As they do so, the light is reflected off them, showing up the darkness around. As they see the light reflected, some who sit in darkness choose to enter the light. In this way, the beam of light extends its influence, but the edge of its circle of light remains clearly defined.[7]

To Live in the Light

We expose our own sins to the light by confessing them to the Giver of light. He already sees them, of course, but we need to see them for what they are in the light of his truth. If we hide them in the darkness, they fester. God's light brings healing.

The light of God also exposes the darkness around us. That does not mean that Christians should run around pointing fingers at children of darkness; it does mean that our very presence should bring into any situation the light of Christ. He will do the exposing. And God's light can bring healing.

You see, the light of Christ makes evil visible not just to condemn it but to make healing possible. Sometimes that hurts, but the quickest way to healing is never to ignore the disease. The quickest way to healing is to allow the Great Physician access to the wound.

God's light leads the way to healing and wholeness.

Sometimes the first step to healing is simply to wake up to the need for it! Paul reminds his readers of what may be a little verse from an early baptismal hymn: "Wake up, O sleeper, rise from the dead, and Christ will shine on you" (5:14).

As the story goes, a mother was once trying to console her little girl after the death of the family's cat. The mom meant well but was mistaken, I think, in more ways than one when she told her daughter, "Tabby's in heaven now."

The little girl grappled with that thought for a moment, and then she asked, "Mommy, why would God want a dead cat?"[8]

Good point. Which makes me wonder—why would God want dead disciples? I'm sure he doesn't. Others may live in darkness and death, asleep to God's goodness, but God's people wake up into the new life of Christ. They rise from death to life, and the sun of the light of Christ shines in their lives and lights their way.

What does a Christian who is "walking as a child of light" look like?

In a nutshell, that Christian looks like a person who is becoming more and more like the Lord he or she serves. He's not a man who never sins—there are none of those—but he is a man who confesses his sins to the Father and to fellow travelers who love the Lord, so that what would fester in the darkness is brought into the light for healing. She is a woman with the life of Christ living inside and cleansing her from every sin. They are people who are being true to their baptism, who in baptism really did die to sin as they died with Christ and were reborn to new life.

There are some advantages to being dead, you know.

Dead people don't pay taxes! The IRS can't touch 'em!

As Christian people, we've died to sin. It's to have no more sway in our lives than the IRS would have in the life of a dead man!

I know we feel the pull of temptation at times, and all too often we fall. We're still living in a world ruled by Satan, but we must never forget that we're not his.

We're not children of darkness. We're children of light.

We're to consider ourselves dead to sin and alive to Christ. We're to be true to our profession of faith, true to our baptism, true to our Lord, living as people who really have been forgiven of all our sins and empowered to live new lives to the glory of God.

It was after his impassioned and impromptu and, perhaps he is now thinking, improvident, speech to the Pharisees, that the newly-sighted man of John 9, born blind, finds himself outside the synagogue. Reborn but cast out.

Word of his excommunication spread, maybe almost as quickly as word of his healing. But the word found its way to *the* Word.

I'd love to have seen the next beautiful scene the apostle of love recounts later in John 9.

Jesus searches for the once-blind man, finds him, and stands before him. The Lord has a question for him.

"Do you believe in the Son of Man?"

And the surprised man answers, "Who is he, sir? Tell me so that I may believe in him."

Jesus says, "You have now seen him. In fact, he is the one speaking with you."

Perhaps it is in those last few words that the light begins to dawn in this man's life yet again, and he begins to recognize the voice he'd heard but the face he'd never seen. He realizes that he is seeing the man who had healed him by opening his eyes to the light.

And he falls at his feet.

And he says, "Lord, I believe."

And he worships him.

So, I pray, may we.

Chapter 11

Be very careful, then, how you live–not as unwise but as wise, making the most of every opportunity, because the days are evil. Therefore do not be foolish, but understand what the Lord's will is. Do not get drunk on wine, which leads to debauchery. Instead, be filled with the Spirit. Speak to one another with psalms, hymns and spiritual songs. Sing and make music in your heart to the Lord, always giving thanks to God the Father for everything, in the name of our Lord Jesus Christ.

Ephesians 5:15-20

When You're Walking
in Dangerous Territory

Be very careful, then,
how you live—
not as unwise but as wise, . . .
EPHESIANS 5:15

When you're walking in dangerous territory, it pays to keep your eyes open. We are, and we'd better. I'll never forget the day, years ago now, when my middle sons, Jeffrey and Stephan, and a couple of their friends, were heading for one of their favorite bike-riding spots. Located just on the outskirts of town in the middle of a pasture, within easy walking or biking distance from our neighborhood, it's a big caliche pit known affectionately by all the neighborhood kids simply as THE PIT.

THE PIT is a big hole in the ground filled with bike trails, hills, jumps, etc. It's not too far off from home, but far enough off. It's not totally out of reach of parents, but far enough out of reach. It's not like screaming down the rim of the Grand Canyon on a motocross bike, but it's close enough that a good imagination can supply what's lacking. And normally, from the local parents' perspective, it's relatively safe.

But the Pit, or at least the path to the Pit, wasn't safe on that Thursday.

Jeffrey, his brother, and his buddies were crossing the road at the end of the pavement to head down to the Pit. He took a step, heard a strange sound, looked down, and discovered that he'd planted his foot right on the business end of a rattlesnake.

How to Measure a Rainbow

The only good thing I can think of about rattlesnakes is that God tagged 'em. Right on the tail.

Dogs may wag their tails to show affection; affection is not what rattlesnakes have in mind. Jeffrey didn't have to think twice to know that this critter's tail-wag meant he was not at all pleased to have his head under the big foot of a human who'd strayed into his territory.

Upon sober reflection, it might have occurred to Jeffrey that the real problem at hand was how to get off the serpent's noggin without getting bit once its mouth was free. I can imagine myself standing there for a good long time not much happier than the snake in a mutually unpleasant situation with neither of us knowing how to gracefully and safely take his leave.

In hindsight, though, since his way of getting off worked, I'm glad Jeffrey didn't stop to cogitate as long as I might have. He got off that snake even more quickly than he'd gotten on! Human boy went one way, rattle-tailed reptile went the other, and both were glad to get away intact.

I doubt I need to say more to impress upon you that Jeffrey had a close call that day. If he'd stepped on the other end of that snake, the day's events would very likely have ended much differently. As it happened, a rattlesnake with a headache may have favored our kids with a very valuable lesson: The Pit may seem pretty friendly, but our kids—and all the kids in the neighborhood—now know for sure that they're not the only living things that move around down there, and that not all the inhabitants are friendly. When you're walking in dangerous territory, it pays to keep your eyes open.

Not a Safe Place

We are, by the way. This world is not a safe place to live. Ever since our First Parents in Eden got snakebit and Paradise fell to sin's venomous poison, this world has been a rough neighborhood with lots of dangers worse than rattlesnakes.

People get hurt here.

Some are just walking along on the journey and the snake strikes. Little kids get leukemia.

Families get broken.

Daddies get laid off.

Dreams get shattered.

People get hurt.

Just in the last few days, just in my little town, I stood at a graveside with a friend who was burying her father. I worried with some other friends about test results and futures and finances (and I worried about the poor showing I was making trying to follow the biblical injunction against worrying). I felt the sick, helpless feeling that came when I learned that a good woman and her family were dealing with the deplorably consistent laws of physics which say that even good people who don't deserve to get hurt do when heavy objects like automobiles roll over.

People get hurt here.

Some get bit by snakes they try to pick up and play with. Pick up a good load of materialism and greed, start running life on the fast track to keep up with the "haves" and disdain the "have nots," and you'll eventually drop out of the race snakebit. Lay a hand on adultery and it'll bite you every time. Mess around with hatred and bitterness and other venom of that sort too long and you needn't be surprised when you end up poisoned.

Whether you're bit because you simply stepped on the wrong end of the serpent as you were passing through on your journey or you got envenomated because you foolishly messed with the wrong reptile, the bites hurt.

This world is not a safe place. Not since Eden fell. People get hurt here.

How to Measure a Rainbow

Enemy-occupied territory. That's the term C. S. Lewis used to describe this enemy-occupied world. Christians believe, he writes, that "an evil power has made himself for the present the Prince of this World." But, he continues, "Christianity is the story of how the rightful king has landed, you might say landed in disguise, and is calling us all to take part in a great campaign of sabotage."[1]

You can take part in the great "underground" resistance movement in lots of ways, but they are all related to swearing allegiance to the rightful King and living out in actions large and small your vows to do him honor.

"When you go to church," Lewis writes, "you are really listening-in to the secret wireless [radio] from our friends: that is why the enemy is so anxious to prevent us from going."[2] There might well be an important message from Heaven there! The enemy would rather we not get it.

When you perform a simple act of kindness for someone who couldn't possibly pay you back, when you resolve to ask for heavenly help to lay aside a resentment that's been smoldering for years, when you do your very best not just for you but for the God who made you—then you show unmistakably the colors of the King, and the enemy sees one more sign that his days are numbered and that his downfall is sure.

It *is* sure, you know. When the Prince of Peace died on the cross and defeated death, he sealed the doom of the Prince of Darkness. The warrant for his death is signed in blood and was served on a cross. The date for his execution is set. And he will die. Of that you may be sure.

The time will come when Satan will be a toothless serpent, a banished enemy, but right now Satan is still loose and he's still dangerous. He's enraged to know that he's in a battle he cannot win, but he takes demonic delight in inflicting all the pain and suffering he can while this world is still his. This world is still enemy-occupied territory, and the enemy is still dangerous.

We can't afford to forget that, if we're on the side of the rightful King, the victory is already ours. And what a victory celebration we'll share with Christ when he comes! But neither can we afford to be anything less than vigilant while we're behind the lines and the enemy is still on the loose. Live soldiers are the ones who don't forget they're in a war. Who don't turn their backs on the enemy. Who aren't caught by surprise. Who haven't allowed apathy to lull them to sleep at their posts.

People still get hurt here. Too many. Too often. When you're walking in dangerous territory, it pays to keep your eyes open.

May I make a few suggestions for how to make a successful trip through this enemy-occupied territory?

Keep Your Eyes Open

First of all, since it is indeed dangerous out here, keep your eyes open and be alert.

I love the story of the little old man and his wife who were on a train trip years ago when friends convinced them to take their very first taste of a soft drink. They'd never tried a carbonated beverage, and it seemed like a good time. But just as the old fellow put the bottle to his lips and downed a tentative swig, the train went into a pitch-black tunnel, and, horrified, he yelled, "Don't drink that sody pop, Marthy! It'll make ye blind as a bat!"

Folks, when you're walking through dangerous territory, and we are, you can't afford to walk through blind. When it's dark, keep your eyes open—and be on the lookout for some helpful light.

How to Measure a Rainbow

My wife and I got a great deal on a new sectional sofa sleeper unit the other day. New to us, at least. It was high time, I'll have to admit!

That is indeed an admission on my part since I hate to spend money on furniture. Among the biggest financial hits we've ever absorbed have occurred at furniture stores. I look forward to going to furniture stores like I'd look forward to going back to the scene of a terrible accident!

And what, after all, does the stuff *do*? I'd far rather put denarii into something that'll crunch data, process words, and even tell you good morning on the screen if you program it right. I wanted, you can tell, to upgrade the computer. My wife said that would happen only if it was one you could sit on.

A computer or a couch. It should have been an easy decision. Since we couldn't afford either, it really should have been neither.

But even I had to admit that it was time and past for some new furniture. The old re-covered couch was coming apart and a canyon had been created at one end where its old springs had just given up and splayed out. Besides that, we needed a sofa sleeper. Our only other beds bigger than a single are water beds. Some of our honored occasional guests are in their eighties, and eighty-year-olds, we reasoned, shouldn't be expected to navigate waterbeds! So we bought the sectional sofa sleeper with all its attendant pieces.

But we immediately discovered a problem. For this new furniture to fit into the room just as it really should, in the very best way, in the optimum arrangement, either the sectional would have to be trimmed four inches or the room expanded the same amount. No amount of pushing, shoving, and sweating could compress the overstuffed thing the requisite four inches.

So we went to Plan B. Actually, to Plan B-Z and beyond.

When You're Walking in Dangerous Territory

Because, after the single optimum configuration was no longer an option, there seemed to be about a thousand other ways the thing could possibly be configured. I'm convinced we saw them all.

Finally, we decided on one arrangement and invited friends over to eat and celebrate. They walked in the door, and I could see the wheels turning. Once again, the furniture started moving. We tried several more configurations—and then put it back the way it was—which was really not too bad, we decided.

The only problem with the way it was—and is—is that the chaise lounge section sort of sticks out a bit into the walkway through the living room. It's not too bad, really. It's just different. And it's no problem at all during the daytime. But so far every time I've moseyed through the living room in the darkness of night, I've come within inches of walking right into the thing and ending up with my nose nailed to the floor!

Darkness can make traveling treacherous even in a safe living room. And this world is not safe! You can't afford to walk through it in the darkness.

So my first suggestion to you for traveling safely through enemy-occupied territory has been this: Keep your eyes open, and be sure you have a light.

The Light of the World is the Son. Walk through this world with him. He's walked through it before, and he's the very best Guide. Follow him. Don't take your eyes off of him. Listen to him. And let him lead.

The psalmist wrote long ago, and I can't say the words without hearing Amy Grant's clear tones, "Thy word is a lamp unto my feet and a light unto my eyes."[3] Read it. Listen to it. Receive it. Make it part of your life and travel by its light. It's one very real way Christ will help you get through dark and dangerous territory.

Remember, You Don't Belong Here!

My next suggestion to you is this: When in this enemy-occupied world the rough times do come, when you've been stung and you're feeling the poison, or when you've been bruised in the battle and you wonder when and if it will ever end, remember that you don't belong here.

It is neither the best music nor the best poetry, but the old song is right on target when it reminds me, "This world is not my home; I'm just a-passing through!"[4] That indeed being the case, it doesn't make too much sense for us to get too attached to what is simply transitory.

That's not pessimism; it's reality. That's not cynicism; it's truth.

I'm not within a thousand miles of suggesting that the best way not to get hurt is to refuse to feel. I'm not at all saying that, because one day we'll be called to leave this world behind, we shouldn't allow ourselves to love what is good even in this fallen world that is still so replete with reflections of God's beauty.

I am saying, be careful where you focus.

If you focus on the earthbound, your hopes end up buried in earth's dirt as all of your dreams take only shallow root. If you focus on the heavenly, your eyes are lifted upward and you find that you can see a lot that's heavenly right here even in a world that's been seriously broken and twisted.

But when what you see around you in this world is not so beautiful, when you see the hurt and you see the pain, let it remind you that this is neither the world God intended nor the world he designed. His specifications didn't include goatheads and grassburs, or sin and death. It's a world that is fallen. It's a world that is not really your home.

One summer some years ago while I was away for a week preaching at a loving and lovely little church in Indiana, one of the leaders there who is an avid golfer took my son Jeffrey and me out for a round of golf. Indiana is a beautiful state filled with rolling hills and lush green lawns and meadows. And, to a Texas flatlander's eye, even the public golf courses, at least the ones I saw, are gorgeous.

As we were making our way around the course, we came over a hill. I looked across the fairway and there, a discreet distance out of the line of fire, nestled down in a wonderfully green meadow surrounded by verdant trees, was a fabulous three-story home under construction. The term "mansion" would be little exaggeration. It was beautiful.

Below the mansion, just a stone's throw down the hill, was a small mobile home, modest by anyone's standards. My friend Irvin explained to me that the owners of the golf course were building a new home right on the course. That new home was the mansion. But until its completion, the owners were living in the mobile home.

I have no doubt that the little trailer provided shelter from the elements about as well as the mansion soon would. But, folks, when you've got a mansion waiting, it doesn't make too much sense to get too attached to an edifice one notch above a fold-out camp trailer!

When you're feeling the pain this enemy-occupied world can inflict, remember you've got a mansion waiting! That being the case, it doesn't make much sense to get too attached down here. For God's child, this is not home. Not really.

You needn't worry about leaving it. You don't need to look back because, and I'm absolutely sure of this, when we go home, really home, home where we belong with the Father, we'll not be leaving anything worthwhile behind.

If it's good here, it will be there and in far greater supply. If it brings you joy here, something will be there which gives you that same joy but magnified a million times.

What do you like to see? Do you love to watch a beautiful sunset? The sun won't set in Heaven, but I promise you there will be color and beauty there to dwarf the brightest sunset this world has ever seen.

What do you like to do? Do you love to ski? I do, and I can tell you truthfully that I've never felt more suddenly and amazingly close to God than when I found myself suddenly and amazingly out of control on skis! Just kidding.

But, no kidding, something is gloriously beautiful about the view from the top of a majestic mountain and the pristine purity of the snow, and I love the exhilaration of heading down a hill and thrilling to God's creation all the way down the mountain. I'm not sure there'll be snow and slopes in Heaven, but I'm absolutely sure something will be there that gives the same joy but immeasurably increased and completely unfiltered, totally untainted.

And who do you love here as purely and deeply as earth allows? Magnify that love a trillion times and try to imagine the joy of knowing each other absolutely completely and fully with nothing at all held back, and you may have caught just the smallest glimpse of what awaits.

All of the best glimmers of goodness and joy that we've known in this fallen world, and we've known a lot that is incredibly good and gives us deep joy, are only muted reflections of the splendorous reality we'll know in Heaven when we come to the Source of all joy.

When we do, I'm convinced we'll find that everything good and lovely in this present world, even the very best this world holds, is only a dim "shadow or copy of what waits for us in our true home."[5] And, when we finally arrive really Home, I believe that the words of the dear Unicorn in The Last Battle, the final book in C. S. Lewis' wonderful children's books, The Chronicles of Narnia, will be our words: "I have come home at last! This is my real country! I belong here. This is the land I have been looking for all my life, though I never knew it till now."[6]

Even in a dangerous world, enemy-occupied territory, much remains that's wonderfully good. But remember—all the time, but especially when you're hurting—that right now you're in the house trailer. There's a mansion that's waiting. Don't settle for too little too soon. This world is not your home. You're just passing through. Something far better, far more real and substantial and permanent, awaits.

Get Drunk!

My final suggestion to you for making the trip through dangerous territory is one you'll hardly believe. I daresay it will be advice you've never heard before from a preacher, and you probably won't again, but my third suggestion to you is this: Get drunk.

I am absolutely convinced that the best way to make it through this world is drunk. So, get drunk! As quickly as you can. As thoroughly as you can. Totally soused. Completely under the influence. Drink deeply and drain the cup.

Get drunk as you drink deeply of God's Spirit.

Believe it or not, that's exactly what Paul is saying in Ephesians 5. He's making a contrast. Don't get drunk with wine as you make your way through a dark and dangerous world. Yes, "the days are evil," but don't get drunk with wine "which leads to debauchery" and compounds the evil and makes a bad situation worse. Instead, "be filled with the Spirit" which leads to singing and praise, thanksgiving and joy, in your hearts to God!

Don't try to anesthetize your soul as you focus on a sick and fallen world; open your eyes wide to the beauty of the Creator and the wonderful ways he brings healing.

Get drunk on wine and you start seeing double. Pretty soon it's double the hurt. Double the pain. Drink deeply of the Spirit and more clearly than ever before you'll start seeing God's beauty and you'll experience his healing.

Get drunk on wine and you wander around confused, stumbling, not knowing which way to go. Drink deeply of the Spirit and you'll find direction and a Guide for the journey.

Get drunk on wine and you might sing bawdy songs in the darkness of a dirty, dingy dive. Drink deeply of God's Spirit and in your heart will well up songs of praise and thanksgiving.

Get drunk enough on wine and your body will rebel and try to vomit out the poison. Drink deeply of the Spirit and your soul will overflow with the refreshing streams of God's joy.

"Don't get drunk on wine, . . . be filled with the Spirit" (5:18). Get drunk! And may you drink deeply and often!

A Real Enemy

Our enemy is real. This world really *is* enemy-occupied territory. The enemy would love for you to stumble through it blind, drunk with pain.

C. S. Lewis, after he'd written about the spiritual warfare that really is going on in this world, wrote that someone always seems to ask, "Do you really mean, at this time of day, to re-introduce our old friend the devil—hoofs and horns and all?"

Lewis' reply was this: "Well, what the time of day has to do with it I do not know. And I am not particular about the hoofs and horns. But in other respects my answer is 'Yes, I do.' I do not claim to know anything about his personal appearance. If anybody really wants to know him better I would say to that person, 'Don't worry. If you really want to, you will. Whether you'll like it when you do is another question.'"[7]

When You're Walking in Dangerous Territory

It's not a lot of fun to feel the need to point out snakes and to remind energetic youngsters that they can't just go running through seemingly safe fields with complete abandon. But somebody needs to say it: The "field" where we live and work and play is not a safe place. When you're walking through dangerous territory, it pays to keep your eyes open.

After Jeffrey and his rattlesnake friend parted company, the snake slithered off across an alley and into a neighbor's back yard. Just inside their yard is a little child's playhouse complete with toys and dolls, and I could just imagine an innocent little one toddling into the playhouse and right into the fangs of an already angry rattlesnake.

When folks are in that kind of danger, you warn them. When I learned about the snaky incident and the situation at hand, I phoned our neighbors. Nobody was home, so I left a message on their answering machine. And, just to be sure they got the message, I went over and taped a note to the door.

God's taped a note to our door, too. You're walking through dangerous territory, he warns. The days are evil. It pays to keep your eyes open.

If you look down, you'll find that the pain and hurt, the sin and wickedness of this world, are real and substantial. But, if you remember to look up, you'll find that God is the ultimate reality. And God is far more substantial.

The good news right now is this: If you really want to know God and his marvelous power and ultimate protection better, you can. If you really want to drink deeply of his abiding and indwelling Spirit, you will.

And I promise that you'll like it when you do!

Chapter 12

Submit to one another out of reverence for Christ.
Wives, submit to your husbands as to the Lord. For the husband is the head of the wife as Christ is the head of the church, his body, of which he is the Savior. Now as the church submits to Christ, so also wives should submit to their husbands in everything.
Husbands, love your wives, just as Christ loved the church and gave himself up for her to make her holy, cleansing her by the washing with water through the word, and to present her to himself as a radiant church, without stain or wrinkle or any other blemish, but holy and blameless. In this same way, husbands ought to love their wives as their own bodies. He who loves his wife loves himself. After all, no one ever hated his own body, but he feeds and cares for it, just as Christ does the church—for we are members of his body. "For this reason a man will leave his father and mother and be united to his wife, and the two will become one flesh." This is a profound mystery—but I am talking about Christ and the church. However, each one of you also must love his wife as he loves himself, and the wife must respect her husband.
Children, obey your parents in the Lord, for this is right. "Honor your father and mother"—which is the first command- ment with a promise—"that it may go well with you and that you may enjoy long life on the earth."
Fathers, do not exasperate your children; instead, bring them up in the training and instruction of the Lord.
Slaves, obey your earthly masters with respect and fear, and with sincerity of heart, just as you would obey Christ. Obey them not only to win their favor when their eye is on you, but like slaves of Christ, doing the will of God from your heart. Serve wholeheartedly, as if you were serving the Lord, not men, because you know that the Lord will reward everyone for what- ever good he does, whether he is slave or free.
And masters, treat your slaves in the same way. Do not threaten them, since you know that he who is both their Master and yours is in heaven, and there is no favoritism with him.

Ephesians 5:21-6:9

The Servant King

Submit to one another out of reverence for Christ. . . .
Serve wholeheartedly, as if you were serving the Lord, not men, . . .
EPHESIANS 5:21, 6:7

A s I was walking through the White House the other day, I received a very nice, though somewhat shocking, surprise. As I meandered down the ground-floor corridor on my way to the State Dining Room, I wandered past the Vermeil Room and the Library—and past old Auguste Rodin's famous sculpture "The Thinker," still lost in thought in the garden exhibit just beyond the corridor windows. No big surprise there. I was deep in thought myself.

I continued on up the stairs to the State floor and made my way through the East Room where seven Presidents have lain in state, past the very grand Steinway piano boasting ivories once tickled quite proficiently by President Harry Truman, then into and through the Green Room under the ever-watchful eyes of Louisa Catherine Adams, John Quincy's wife whose portrait graces the lushly-papered green walls but who seemed hardly surprised at all to see me.

Time was getting by, and I was beginning to be in something of a hurry.

You don't need to tell me that security at the White House needs to be quite high, but it does look like the Secret Service would learn to be just a bit faster at the gate.

Anyway, I rushed on through the newly-refurbished but

always elegant Blue Room with its gilded furniture, the graceful chairbacks sporting silk upholstery and gold eagle medallions. I flew through the Red Room and its red twill satin-covered walls, the room which, before it was red, was regular witness to the indomitable Dolley Madison's fashionable Wednesday night receptions. Dolley was nowhere around to register any surprise at my presence.

But I simply must be more careful in the future because when I burst through the doorway into the State Dining Room, I almost ran right over a fairly good-sized fellow clad in old overalls. Stooped over holding a dust rag in one hand and a can of furniture polish in the other, he looked up at me, and a momentary flicker of surprise flashed across his face before he smiled a little tiredly and intoned, "Oh, hi! Sorry, but I didn't see you coming."

"No problem," I said, pausing to catch my breath. "I didn't know anybody was scheduled to work in here today and so you sort of surprised me, but I should have been paying more attention, and I'll try to be more careful in the future. Say, how long have you been working here?"

"Well," he looked up at me again, "if you mean how long in the White House, sometimes it seems like just about forever. But if you mean right here in the State Dining Room, only a few hours. You see, I've got a Cabinet meeting up in the Oval Office in an hour or so, and I'll be busy getting coffee and tea for everybody. I'd asked the guys earlier if anybody'd be willing to do some dusting in here. Big reception tonight. Some Middle Eastern sheik or somebody. Black tie stuff, and I don't want anybody going away dusty. None of the Cabinet folks seemed too excited about dusting, though, and I'll probably be a little too busy to do it later since I'm the President and all."

Well, you could've knocked me over with a dust mop! My jaw fell.

"Mr. President?"

"Uh, well, yeah."

"*The* President?"

"Don't look like myself, huh?"

But, yes, now that he mentioned it, forget the paint-spattered and dust-covered overalls and lose the dusting rag, and . . . well, for goodness' sakes!

"Oh, don't look so surprised. This old room needed a little dusting. Somebody had to do it, and, aw, shoot! I'm not too high and mighty to do a little domestic work!

"You know, they call this place the White House. Seems to me if they'd try using a little more white inside and maybe a few pastels instead of all these really dark colors, we might get away with a little less dusting.

"Say, is there something I can do for you? Would you like a glass of tea or something?"

Well, *that*, ladies and gentlemen, was quite an experience. Color me surprised!

And color me even more surprised if you believe any of this.

Now, to be perfectly honest, which is not exactly what I've been for the past few paragraphs, I was indeed in Washington recently. I did indeed walk through part of the White House. In fact, I spent a little time in or near every room I've just described, and, thank you for asking, it was an absolutely fine experience.

But I wasn't alone. Not even nearly. I stood in one of the longest lines I've ever seen for more than an hour with hundreds of people of all sorts all waiting to walk through the President's house. And we all did. (I don't believe I'd want to live in my house if my house was everybody's house.)

It was neat.

It was exciting.

It was interesting.

But he wasn't there (and that particular President is not there now because the White House will have new residents by the time you read this). I think he was in an Asia-Pacific leaders' conference in New Zealand or somewhere rubbing noses with some of the thugs from China. In any case, the President wasn't home when I visited his house. And (surprise!) he surely wasn't home dusting any of the furniture.

But part of my story was true, you see, and this much is also true—I'd be really surprised to go to the White House and find the President doing the dusting. I didn't expect to see Auguste Rodin's "Thinker" out in the Jacqueline Kennedy Garden, but I certainly wouldn't expect to look through the window and see the President out hoeing the weeds around the sculptural exhibit (by the way, there weren't any weeds) or perched on top of a Toro riding lawn mower cutting the grass. It just wouldn't be, well, presidential.

Well, would it?

I don't think I would want the leader of the free world spending a lot of time doing housework. Somebody, lots of somebodies, spends lots of time taking care of his house, and that's an important and worthwhile job. But the President's job is more important, and he needs to spend his time focusing on that job.

No, dusting is just not particularly presidential.

But, surprisingly enough, it might be better than presidential. It might even be divine.

The Servant of All

On the scale of domestic activities, dusting is certainly no more humbling than footwashing. I've never seen a President doing the dusting. But I've seen the word-pictures painted by Gospel writers who tell of the divine Son of God draping himself in a towel, dipping his hands into a basin, and deliberately and graciously washing the dust-streaked feet of his disciples.[1]

Oh, we're surprised by that. But certainly no more than they were! They were horrified that their Master would stoop to become the servant of them all. And the volume of their horror would increase to become a shrill cacophony when just hours later they would see his beautiful hands bleeding and remember the gentle touch of those hands—strong hands that helped fling the stars across the canvas of the universe, loving hands deftly wrapped around feet that were too often wayward, the feet of followers who were slow to understand and slower still to serve.

And, later, rewinding the mental video of that surreal scene, they might well wonder: On that night had anyone remembered or bothered to wash *his* feet?

Or was the salty sacrifice of tears and the hair-toweled tender anointing of the weeping woman at the home of Simon the Pharisee still the most fitting washing for the feet of Jesus the Christ, the Messiah, God's Anointed One?[2]

Or would the real washing of his feet come later as the precious drops of his life drained out and drop by drop pooled to become crimson rivers streaking downward, sufficient to carry away the dust from his feet, all-sufficient to wash away the sin from our lives?

Ah, but we are so surprised when the Son of God, who you would certainly think had more important things to do, especially on the last night of his life, decides that the very thing which must be done, the most important thing he can do, the highest work of all at that holy time on that holy evening, is to wash the feet of his disciples.

Sore feet? Maybe.

Sore disciples? Surely.

How to Measure a Rainbow

I really hate to mess with the picture, you know. DaVinci's great painting. Your own mental conception of the scene. But the Gospel accounts leave no doubt. The disciples were pretty sore that night. They'd just been fussing about who was greatest in the Kingdom. When Jesus came into his Kingdom, who would become Secretary of State? Which apostles would have cabinet rank? They were looking, so to speak, for offices in the Jerusalem White House. Not one apostle wanted a dead-end career in housekeeping dusting baseboards. Nobody wanted to be a servant.[3]

The disciples thought foot-washing was servant's work. Not surprising.

What is eternally surprising is that the Lord thought so, too. Foot-washing was indeed servant's work. It was work for the Servant of all. It was God's work.

Some work only God is powerful enough to do. Some work only God is willing to stoop low enough to do.

God the Son stepped down from the right hand of God the Father and wrapped in swaddling cloths at Bethlehem stooped to enter our world.

Jesus the Christ stepped down from the place of honor and wrapped in a servant's towel at the Last Supper stooped to wash the disciples' dirty feet.

The Lamb of God, the Son of God, stepped down from the Holy of Holies and wrapped in our sin and our guilt stooped to lie down on a cross.

And we watch. The disciples then. The disciples now. And Heaven and all its angelic hosts. The incongruity of the perfect serving the utterly imperfect, the obscenity of the totally pure allowing himself to be poisoned by the venom of the impure, strikes us with such force that everything within us screams, "This must not be!"

But Christ's voice of thunder is already becoming a

newborn's cry. Jesus' soon-to-be bleeding hand is even now reaching down to grasp the basin. The Son of God is rushing toward eclipse as a Roman soldier's hand is raised around a hammer rushing toward a terrible nail.

And the Voice of all love, mercy, and grace, full to overflowing with all joy and all sorrow, speaks in divine gentleness more powerful than all earthly might, "This *must* be."

The spectacle of the President of the United States dusting woodwork? That is less than insignificant compared to the spectacle of the Author of Life dying on a cross.

Asking the Wrong Questions

Now what, pray tell, does all of this, as marvelously wonderful as it is, have to do with the Apostle Paul's words and the Holy Spirit's wisdom as revealed in these verses from Ephesians 5 and 6?

Much!

Have you ever noticed how prone we are to asking the wrong questions?

We're like the religious lawyer in Luke 10. When Christ pointed him to the heart of the Law, "'Love the Lord your God with all your heart and with all your soul and with all your strength and with all your mind'; and, 'Love your neighbor as yourself'" (v. 27), he wanted some additional explication.

What he really wanted, according to Luke, was "to justify himself" (v. 29). As Eugene Peterson paraphrases, this lawyer was "looking for a loophole" when he asked Jesus, "Who is my neighbor?"[4] His question became the occasion for the Lord's telling of the parable of the Good Samaritan.

"Who is my neighbor?" What he is asking is this: Who has just claim to my love? Who am I obligated to love? Just people next door or folks three houses down? Just those living fifty feet from my property line or even those who live around the block? What's the law on this? What, and let me get this in writing, is my legal obligation? After all, you'd hate to waste a lot of time and energy loving someone you don't really have to love!

He was asking the wrong question. But Jesus, with a marvelous story, asks and answers the right one—not "Who is my neighbor?" but "How can I *be* a neighbor to those in need, all of whom are my neighbors and have just claim to my mercy?"

We ask the wrong questions.

We're like Peter who came to Jesus wanting to know how many times he had to forgive a brother's transgression against him.

"Lord, how often shall my brother sin against me, and I forgive him?"[5]

Peter thought he already knew. He'd given the matter serious thought, and seven times seemed a more than reasonable, even magnanimous and generous-hearted, answer. After all, we shouldn't go to extremes. Let's pick a reasonable number of times for forgiveness to be extended and then perhaps add a couple of times to show that we're the right sort, and then let's start counting!

"Let's Make a Deal" may be the television show but "Let's Make a Law" is the game we're playing when we're asking the wrong questions, most of which are prompted by our pathetic attempts at *self*-justification.

Jesus astounds Peter by appealing to the law of love. Not seven times but "seventy times seven" times![6] I believe he was saying "times without number."[7] You don't make a law. You don't keep a record. You don't even begin to count. Because the right question is not "How many times do I have to forgive?" No, the right question is "How many times have I been forgiven?" And, maybe, "How many times do I wish to be?"

The Servant King

Still we persist in asking the wrong questions.

We're like the angry family member who wanted Jesus to practice family law. He recognized a rabbi when he saw one. He felt the authority with which Jesus taught, and he wanted the weight of that authority on his side.

"Teacher," he intoned indignantly, "tell my greedy brother to divide the family inheritance with me!"[8]

And Jesus answered, "Mister, what makes you think it's any of my business to be a judge or mediator for you?" And then he said to the people, "'Take care! Protect yourself against the least bit of greed. Life is not defined by what you have, even when you have a lot.'"[9]

"What can I do about my brother's greed?" The wrong question.

"What can you help me do about my own greed?" Now, there's the right one.

Sometimes we need more than answers for the questions of our lives. We need help even to ask the right questions—the kind of help Jesus was trying to give religious lawyers and befuddled apostles and even mad family members. The kind of help he'll give you and me if we really want it.

The Right Question Regarding Submission

I'm convinced many of us have come to Paul's words in Ephesians 5 and 6 asking this: "To whom must I grudgingly submit?" It's the wrong question.

And we're just a stone's throw away from asking, with a flame-fueled glimmer in our eye, and devilish eagerness, a question even dearer to the heart of Hell, "Tell me quickly now, who has to submit to *me*?" It is absolutely the wrong question.

We need the Lord's help to ask the right one. I believe that he has already given the help we need, if we'll just look and listen.

How to Measure a Rainbow

In the wonderful words of *Ephesians*, Paul has painted a picture of our universe, our world, and our lives as given meaning, direction, and purpose because of what God has done for us through Jesus Christ by uniting us all under him as the Head of the Body, the Church.

Through Christ's death, we die and are pardoned.

Through Christ's resurrection, we are raised and empowered.

Through the Spirit, we are united as God's people, Christ's church. Since the barrier between God and man has come down, now the old seemingly insurmountable barriers between Jew and Gentile (and any other barrier you'd care to mention—racial, social, economic) have also come down.

Before God through Christ united us one with another, we spent a lot of time fussing and fighting, bickering and biting.

Were we Gentiles? What could we do to subjugate Jews and gain the upper hand?

Were we rich? What could we do to further impoverish the poor and grasp more wealth?

Were we white or black or brown? What could we do to humiliate those on the other side of the color chart?

Before Christ united us, we shed blood and sweat and tears trying to claw our way to the top as individuals or as members of our group.

But that was B.C. That was "Before Christ."

That was before Christ stooped to unite us by washing our feet with his own blood. Before Christ showed the depth of his love by reaching unimaginably down to lift us up. Before Christ paid the price to purchase our salvation. And now, everything is changed.

Now, since we as God's people have been filled with the Spirit of God and given new life, our relationships have taken on new life, too.

Earlier in Ephesians 5, Paul draws a stark contrast when he

warns us not to be given over to the influence of alcohol, but instead to be filled with, completely under the influence of, the Spirit. Instead of being drunk with wine, we're to "drink the Spirit of God, huge draughts of him!"[10] And I'm told that, in the Greek, this command to "be filled" is immediately followed by a series of participles describing what that in-filling means in very practical terms. People who are filled with God's Spirit spend time "speaking" their joy to one another "with psalms, hymns, and spiritual songs." They spend time "singing" and "making music" in their hearts to God. They spend time continually "giving thanks."[11]

Speaking.

Singing.

Making music.

Giving thanks.

And there is one more item in the apostolic list, and it may surprise you at first. It certainly offends the sensibilities of our world. It seems senseless as it flies in the face of the pseudo-wisdom of our age and our culture. But people who are filled with God's Spirit also spend time . . .

Submitting.

They would rather be humbly last than be rudely first.

They would rather serve than be served.

They would even rather be hurt than be hurtful.

"Submit to one another out of reverence for Christ" (5:21).

Paul goes on to talk about the very practical difference the influence of the Spirit makes in everyday lives and relationships as we "submit to one another," as we're "courteously reverent" to one another, "out of respect for Christ."[12]

He directs his words to us all and points up particularly wives and husbands, children and parents, slaves and masters.

It must be terribly difficult, horribly so at some times and in some places, to be a slave. But a slave in whom God's Spirit lives knows that the real Master for whom he labors and serves is the Lord who draped himself in a towel, reached for the basin, and washed his disciples' feet. And the Christian first-century master? How dare he be harsh with a slave whose service has been invested with dignity by the Servant Lord of all! And, if you have trouble translating into our modern situation what Paul says to slaves and masters, before you punch the time clock or sign payroll checks many more times, you might ask yourself what he would write today to employees and employers. And you might well wonder what galaxies God may one eternal day put under the rule of the custodian who this morning was mopping the floor of the office break room and humming "Amazing Grace."

Are you a child in whom God's Spirit lives? Then you are to serve and obey your parents, honoring them, being the blessing God intended you to be, and you will find yourself blessed both here and hereafter. You can count on it! Once upon a time there was another Child, you know, who so honored his Father and cared so deeply about doing the Father's will that now he reigns in Heaven at the right hand of God the Father, the King. He was willing to be abased, and now he is exalted.

And now, I hope you understand—forgive me, please—I'd hoped to say more about wives and husbands, husbands and wives, but my time is up, my space is gone, and were I preaching, I'd collect my notes and close the Book and intone, Now let us stand and sing.

What? Oh, you'll not let me off that easily.

I was afraid of that.

Husbands, Wives, & Submission

I know you know I know that Paul mentions another relationship here which in our culture is a bit more difficult to handle. Why are Paul's words and the Spirit's wisdom here regarding wives and husbands, husbands and wives, so often the most difficult of these words for us?

Certainly, in large part these words are difficult because of the loud voice of our society. Even in our topsy-turvy culture, most kids acknowledge at least grudgingly some duty to follow their parents' wishes, and most employees recognize the plain truth of the fact that the employer who signs the check also has the right to scribe a few rules.

I suppose there are still tribes in Africa where the man rules the roost regally and his wife or wives live to do his bidding. I've heard of husbands in the East whose wives always walk a respectful distance in the swirling wake of their dust. And I've seen reports from some parts of the Middle East where wives fan out in front of their husbands as they traipse across the desert to deflect any danger that might threaten the life of #1, the potentate, the patriarch.

But need I tell you that's not the world we live in? Not in the West. And I'm not kidding when I say that's not the world I want to live in. (Please dear, honeybunch, sweetheart, don't hit me again! I'll write it right.) Now I *am* kidding.

But nowhere more than in the marriage relationship are we so tempted to come asking absolutely the wrong question, and something about this most precious relationship magnifies our mistake. We read Paul's words about submission, "Submit to one another out of reverence for Christ," and we straightway ask, "To whom do I have to submit?" which our world is quite sure, and we silently think, after all, is another way of asking, "Who do I have to grudgingly serve? Who has a claim to my service?"

It's the wrong question.

It's Jesus taking the towel in hand, bending over, taking one look at Peter's fisherman's feet, throwing the towel down, and saying, "Really, now, do you honestly expect me to wash *those*? I don't have to wash those."

It's the Samaritan bending over the beaten Jew, seeing the blood and gore, grimacing, and spurring his donkey, "I think I'll pass. No Jew in the world has a right to spatter a Samaritan with that much blood. I don't have to demean myself like this."

It's Peter saying, "I've forgiven my offending brother seven times for the same sin, and he's gone and done it again, and, Lord, I've had enough. I've done enough. I've forgiven enough." And it's Jesus agreeing, "Indeed you have. More than enough. Don't lower yourself and enable his behavior. You don't have to forgive again."[13]

It's the wrong question. And because it's the wrong question, we too often come up with all the wrong answers. Some of them are poignantly painful.

He was pretty sure he understood what the Bible said about wives obeying their husbands. He may not have been sure which apostle or writer said it, but he was quite sure it was said.

I don't know how many times she'd been beaten with misused Scripture like a misshapen cruel club, but she felt it happening in my office yet another time, and it was the last straw, the last blow her bloodied and bludgeoned spirit could sustain.

It was years ago now as the normally quiet and gentle lady and her husband sat in my office discussing the marital difficulties that were bringing them to the brink of divorce. Her husband, who knew precious little about the words of Scripture, knew less about its spirit. Or Christ's Spirit, for that matter.

Just how many times she'd been hit in the face by words of Scripture hurled like hurtful bricks, I don't know. I do know that the farthest thing from my mind was to hurl one myself, or to encourage him to hurl any more.

But this passage came up in the shuffle, and he played his trump card.

"Doesn't the Bible say that wives are to obey their husbands?"

I didn't have time, opportunity, or enough knowledge of the Bible just then to tell him that actually the word "obey" is not the word the Scriptures use regarding wives, though it is used with regard to children and slaves, that the word is "submit," and that though it may well indeed involve obedience, the very same word is applied to husbands, wives, and all the rest of God's people (5:21, "Submit to one another out of reverence for Christ") one verse before the one he had just trotted out.[14]

We had barely begun to discuss the words of Scripture when this dear lady's pain absolutely boiled over in a way that was all the more striking because it was so utterly foreign to her gentle spirit. I don't remember what she screamed, but scream she did, as she erupted from the chair. That scream broke the wall of her dammed up emotions. Hot tears splashed down her cheeks, and bitter pain and gall flooded unbidden but unabated after her as she ran down the hall, seeking escape from the pain threatening to drown her.

God's grace brought time for comfort and power for healing, though that marriage, already dead, was later buried.

But I'll never forget the tidal wave of that pain.

How dare we husbands ever misappropriate and prostitute the words of Scripture to cut up and misuse our wives! Don't we see that our job is to wash their feet, not to use them as footstools? Haven't we read far enough in this passage to realize that we husbands are called to the same level of love with regard to our wives that Christ gave to the church as he lay down his very life for her?

Husbands and wives, wives and husbands, is it an oppressive thing "to submit to one another out of reverence for Christ" if wives are absolutely devoted to their husbands' good, and if husbands are willing to daily lay down their lives and their own selfishness because they genuinely love their wives more than life itself?

Husbands, love your wives as Christ loved the church—so deeply that he died for her to make her his. This divine Prince so loved his beloved that he did not deign to consider even life itself too high a price to pay for his Princess Bride. By his sacrifice she's been cleansed and washed, purified and sanctified, made beautiful and blameless, and every glimpse of her brings him joy.

Wives, honor your husbands as the church honors Christ and, seeing reflected in his eyes the love of all eternity, joyfully pledges an eternity of love.

Husbands and wives, wives and husbands, "submit to one another out of reverence for Christ."

To Learn the Right Question, Look at Jesus

And now, do you see? For *me* to read Paul's words and ask, "To whom do *you* have to submit?" is for me to ask the wrong question.

For me to read the apostle's writing and ask, "To whom do *I* have to submit?" is to ask the wrong question and to betray the wrong spirit.

And to even begin to read the wisdom of the Spirit and to ask, "Now, tell me, who has to submit to *me*?" is to become a tool of Hell, not a subject of Heaven.

To learn the right question, just look at the Lord lying in the crib of Bethlehem, the Servant serving with the basin at the Last Supper, and the Christ hanging on the cross of Calvary.

Take even a glimpse of that Lord, and then try to tell me you can imagine Jesus asking, "Oh, Father, who do I have to serve? Who is worthy of my service?"

No. If we truly see Jesus, we'll spend our lives asking the right question, and it will become a prayer: "Lord Jesus, create in me a loving, gentle, and sacrificial spirit that my submission and service to those around me may become through your grace a beautiful reflection of my submission to you. Grant that in all my life and in all my relationships, I may submit to you, the Son who in all things submitted to the Father, for you are the Lord of all and highly exalted because you were willing as the Lord of the towel and the basin to wash our feet and be abased."

I did go to the White House. But I didn't get to glimpse the Oval Office, and I certainly didn't get to see the President dusting the desk. I doubt that happens.

But if you take a peek into God's House, and into the very Throne Room of Heaven, don't be surprised to see sitting at the right hand of the Father, the Son, glorified but still the very image of the Servant who stooped to wash the feet of the disciples at the Last Supper there in Jerusalem and who lowered himself to the cross of Calvary to wash away the sins of disciples even less worthy. Your feet and mine. Your sins and mine.

You remember, of course, that the job of disciples is to follow their Lord—the foot-washing Lord, the towel-bearing Servant, the bleeding Savior—even in, especially in, submission. The power to submit is power God will give us. He asks of us nothing apart from his grace which is at work within us. But I'm pretty sure that means that there are feet all around us we need to be washing.

Whose tired and road-weary feet can I wash today?

Now, there's the right question!

Chapter 13

Finally, be strong in the Lord and in his mighty power. Put on the full armor of God so that you can take your stand against the devil's schemes. For our struggle is not against flesh and blood, but against the rulers, against the authorities, against the powers of this dark world and against the spiritual forces of evil in the heavenly realms. Therefore put on the full armor of God, so that when the day of evil comes, you may be able to stand your ground, and after you have done everything, to stand. Stand firm then, with the belt of truth buckled around your waist, with the breastplate of righteousness in place, and with your feet fitted with the readiness that comes from the gospel of peace. In addition to all this, take up the shield of faith, with which you can extinguish all the flaming arrows of the evil one. Take the helmet of salvation and the sword of the Spirit, which is the word of God. And pray in the Spirit on all occasions with all kinds of prayers and requests. With this in mind, be alert and always keep on praying for all the saints.

Pray also for me, that whenever I open my mouth, words may be given me so that I will fearlessly make known the mystery of the gospel, for which I am an ambassador in chains. Pray that I may declare it fearlessly, as I should.

Tychicus, the dear brother and faithful servant in the Lord, will tell you everything, so that you also may know how I am and what I am doing. I am sending him to you for this very purpose, that you may know how we are, and that he may encourage you.

Peace to the brothers, and love with faith from God the Father and the Lord Jesus Christ. Grace to all who love our Lord Jesus Christ with an undying love.

Ephesians 6:10-24

A Terminator, Too

*Finally, be strong in the Lord
and in his mighty power.
Put on the full armor of God. . . .*
EPHESIANS 6:10-11

Cinch up your seat belt now and hang on to your hat! We're going to talk war.

But this militant discussion will require some jolting shifts between battlefields separated by multiple centuries and entire worlds.

So look sharp and don't dawdle! (Did I mention that you're about to join the army?) I don't want to lose you along the way!

Make no mistake! We are in a battle.

A battle against enemies you can't always see.

A battle against adversaries who have weapons we've dreamed of only in our worst nightmares.

A battle against a foe whose goal is to destroy everything we love that is good and holy.

We are in a battle.

I don't know about you, but that worries me, because I don't feel much like a soldier.

I'm obviously not a jungle-warfare Rambo-type. I might fit into a library pretty well, but not a jungle.

229

How to Measure a Rainbow

I work fairly well with computer disks, but machine gun clips aren't my thing.

I don't fight in jungles in southeast Asia; I fight crab grass in my lawn. And it's winning.

I'm not a Chuck Norris-type whose karate skills make my hands and feet deadly weapons. I'm at my deadliest when I'm putting people to sleep with dull sermons.

I'm not an Arnold Schwarzenegger pitted against a Terminator-type futuristic fighting machine. I don't like fights.[1]

I've never fought in a cold war or a hot war. I've never fought against a Russian or a "red" of any sort, though I know a lot about fighting against red ink in my checkbook.

I fight the battle of the bulge continually, but it's pretty much confined to the area around my waist and has a lot more to do with fighting off a second helping of dessert than it does with fighting in deserts or jungles halfway around the world.

I'm not much of a soldier.

I've known some folks, though, who were.

Most real soldiers, from what I've seen, aren't guts and glory types; they're pretty ordinary people doing pretty ordinary jobs. And the efforts of those ordinary people doing those ordinary jobs all combine to form what can be an extraordinarily effective military machine. Not many Rambos and Norrises, Terminator-types and karate-kings, but lots of folks doing a job and doing it well. Real generals like H. Norman Schwartzkopf will tell you that those are the kinds of folks who win wars.

I have known some soldiers who literally fought tooth and nail, hand to hand, eyeball to eyeball with the enemy in some battles too bloody to describe. That was their job. They did it well. At the price, often, of their own blood.

My wife's father was one of those. So were some of yours. So were some of you.

A Terminator, Too

On the wall at Juana's mother's house is a "shadow box" containing the ribbons and decorations Sgt. Milton E. "Mick" Cotten won in World War II. Purple hearts and oak leaf clusters for lying wounded in the snow in France, kept from bleeding to death from shrapnel wounds only because the frigid temperatures slowed the flow of blood. The *Croix de Guerre*, the French Cross of War, bearing witness to the high honor bestowed on him by a grateful French government. And from his own government, the Bronze Star for valor and courage under fire.

I've never been under fire. Not like that.

You, too, have probably known folks who were. And your experience is likely the same as mine. I've never known a single soldier who really saw battle who had any room left in his imagination for movie-type guts-and-glory glitter and victory-or-death last-stand charges. (My father-in-law had precious little use for generals like Patton.) In fact, in my experience, the closer they were to bloody battle, the less they want to spend much time talking about it. The highest badges of courage they've won are unseen. So are some of the deepest scars.

It's not easy to be a soldier.

But that's what we Christians are called to be.

Because we're in a battle.

A battle of literally cosmic proportions has been raging since Lucifer, the Light Bearer, mounted his campaign to eclipse the Son of Righteousness. Since Eden fell to the Enemy, this little Planet Earth has been the scene of constant warfare.

It still is.

The battle rages on.

And we can't afford to lose.

But, at first glance, defeat in the face of this Enemy seems almost certain.

How to Measure a Rainbow

How can you possibly fight an enemy so strong?
Every war ever fought,
> every drop of blood ever spilt,
>> every lie ever uttered,
>>> is a tilt of the cap in tribute to his dominion.

Every promise ever broken is a bow in his direction.

Every headstone in a million cemeteries bears mute but unmistakable witness to his malice and his power.

How could you ever hope to make even a dent in this enemy's armor? He's just too strong!

Yes, he is.

For you. For me.

To fight alone is to absolutely insure defeat. You'd have about as much success fighting Satan by yourself as you would putting out a nuclear reaction with a spit of tobacco juice!

Or winning the Super Bowl with a 7th-grade football team still trying to figure out if their pads are on backwards.

Or launching the space shuttle with the powder from an old bottle rocket.

Fight alone, and you will lose.

Guaranteed.

Our whole world couldn't fight him alone. On its own, this whole planet was locked in a downward spiral and heading for certain defeat.

Think back to the time before Christ came.

Decade upon decade of warfare lines up behind as far as the mind's eye can see, and stretching on ahead in what seems to be an endless succession of struggle, the battle rages. But suddenly an angelic trumpet blows and a star shoots across the sky like the first heavenly flare heralding the invasion. At its zenith, it bursts into brilliant light, illuminates the fray, and hangs shining in the sky above a Judean village called Bethlehem.

A Terminator, Too

Heaven's assault has begun. An entire world of pain is potential coastline for the landing, but Bethlehem becomes the chosen beachhead. Legions of angels watch in amazement as the King sends only one landing craft.

And it's a manger.

But its occupant is a Prince.

I love Luci Shaw's poetic depiction of the tiny Prince lying in the manger:

> . . . Quiet he lies
> whose vigor hurled
> a universe. He sleeps
> whose eyelids have not closed before.
> His breath (so slight it seems
> no breath at all) once ruffled the dark deeps
> to sprout a world.
> Charmed by doves' voices, the whisper of straw,
> he dreams,
> hearing no music from his other spheres.
> Breath, mouth, ears, eyes,
> he is curtailed
> who overflowed all skies,
> all years.
> Older than eternity,
> now he is new. . . .[2]

The angels sing.

    The shepherds worship.

        The parents wonder.

Old Simeon and aged Anna know a prince when they see one.[3] They've had practice in looking.

And they know this is *the* Prince.

And they know Heaven itself has invaded Planet Earth.

And they know that the world will never be the same.

But it certainly seems the same.

War? What war? A cosmic battle? Who're you kidding? We could go for a good war, the people say.

A war we had some hope of winning.

A war to spill some Roman blood and throw the pagan dogs out on their ears!

A war to win back the land God gave us, the land we keep losing.

Keep your cosmic battles! One good earthly war right here on terra firma, fought in Judean hills, would be war enough if only we could win it!

"If wishes were horses, beggars would ride," and if victories came just for the asking, Judean feet would rest firmly on Roman throats.

But victories don't come so cheaply, so easily.

Still, the people dreamed of victory.

I know they did.

When their firstborn arrived straight from Heaven, Joseph and Mary already knew his name. It was on the early birth announcement that came from the lips of the angel. But when, down the line, they got to pick the names for his half-brothers, they chose Maccabean names, names from the Jewish family of patriots who years before had led a revolt to throw out another pagan foe.

If only it could happen now!

If only.

But one dreary day kept leading right on into another.

Yes, the angels had sung, but then the hosts of Heaven had been posted to other assignments. An angel or two surely would have come in handy, but from all appearances, they were gone.

The shepherds had themselves gone back to herding sheep.

The stable-turned-delivery room was a stable again.

A Terminator, Too

Joseph was back in the carpenter shop.

Simeon and Anna died having seen the Victor but not the victory.

And the Romans? They were still very much a grim presence.

The star had burned out long ago.

Had the invasion fizzled? Where was Heaven as Earth kept right on hurting?

Nothing seemed to change.

But then, thirty years later (a mere blink of Eternity's eyes), water changed to wine at a wedding reception in a little insignificant village called Cana. It was hardly a shot heard round the world, but Heaven was on the move.

A dove carries a message from Heavenly Headquarters. To a baptism!

The Prince heads to the wilderness for survival training in temptation and meets the Enemy head on.

Then it's time to recruit and train the troops. Not a particularly promising lot.

Fishermen. A tax collector. A zealot.

And others remarkable only because they are so absolutely unremarkable.

The battle is underway! No local newspaper boasts headlines screaming, **"IT'S WAR!"**

But it is.

A blind man focuses on his baby daughter for the first time.

A deaf man's ears reverberate with his wife's whispered, "I love you!"

A woman with a once-withered leg runs a race. And wins.

A just-a-minute-ago-dead girl sits up and smiles at her parents.

A little boy's fever breaks.

And demons fall down to grovel and slobber and beg to be banished into suicidal pigs.

How to Measure a Rainbow

At every touch of the Prince's healing hand, Heaven gains precious ground and Hell slinks away in retreat.

The Baptizer, the great forerunner of the King and a prisoner of war in the fray, lies disheartened and defeated on Herod's Death Row, and he sends his disciples to Jesus with a single poignant question, "Are you the One?"[4]

Tell me, he seems to be saying, and my life will be vindicated, and my death will be worthwhile! Are you the One whose coming was foretold, or shall we look for another?

And the answer comes ringing back from the lips of the Lord: "Go and tell John what you see and hear!"

That the blind are thrilling to sunsets.

That the deaf are listening to symphonies of their children's laughter.

That the dead are marvelously raised along with the hopes of their loved ones.

That the poor are rich with the Good News.

That the long-awaited battle is engaged.

That Heaven is on the march and Hell is on the run!

The vast universe has been waiting through all of eternity for the battle that will decide its fate. And now the cosmic battle gathers force and converges on Planet Earth.

Palestine.

A seemingly God-forsaken land becomes the focus of God's army. And the focus narrows to one hill.

Calvary.

And nailed to its brow, with arms stretched out to embrace the pain of this whole world, a cross.

That cross is the crux,
                    the center,
                              the crucial focal point,
of every moment in history, before or since. Everything focuses there. Eternity is eclipsed and all of time centers on one dark day.

A Terminator, Too

Then three days.

    Then blinding light.

        Then victory!

Yes, I know we don't always feel victorious.

Yes, I know that the Enemy, though his doom is now sealed and his fate is now certain, can still make us bleed. In his death throes, he is still dangerous and deadly.

Yes, I know that the foe, even in defeat, is still far too strong for the likes of you and me.

But not for the Captain of our souls.

Not for the Prince who left Heaven's throne to fight on our behalf.

Not for the One who gathered into himself all the fury of Hell, took our transgressions to a tomb, and rose again to prove once and for all that Life is stronger than Death, that Love is stronger than Hate, that Good is stronger than Evil.

Is the Enemy too strong for us? Yes!

Can we possibly stand firm before the power of Hell? No!

We'd be fools to try to fight at all—were it not for the God who stands with us and equips us for battle.

And that, my friend, changes everything.

So how about a change of clothes? You're not a civilian any longer. Put on your armor! You've been called into the service of the King.

Stand your ground with the belt of truth buckled around your waist. As a Roman soldier was preparing for battle, before he put on his armor, and before he buckled on the metal-studded belt from which hung his sword, he would cinch up his loose garments beneath a broad leather apron-like belt that provided support and secured his clothing so that he was ready to maneuver and to fight without being hampered or tripped up by his own robe. The prize belts for which wrestlers fight even today very likely harken back to this kind of warrior's belt.

And for the Christian soldier, the belt that undergirds him and supports him as he prepares for action is the truth of the gospel.[5]

Strap on righteousness as your breastplate. Ah, it's an important piece of armor that protects your very heart! And for the Christian soldier whose heart is to be just and pure, what better breastplate than a quality of life that loves above all else that which is right and good, holy and life-affirming, those things which are nearest and dearest to the warm heart of God?

Fit on your feet the sandals that are "the readiness that comes from the gospel of peace" (6:15). Roman soldiers often wore a kind of "half-boot" as standard equipment for lengthy marches. The bottoms of these military boots could be fitted with spikes for grip and traction. Wearing these boots, a soldier's feet were ready to carry him wherever he needed to go. The Christian soldier must have feet shod and ready to cover many miles to carry wonderful news. His are the wonderfully "beautiful" feet the prophet Isaiah wrote about so many years ago as he blessed the feet of those who carry God's good news.[6] Ironic, isn't it?, that the Christian soldier is prepared for any difficult battle precisely because his heart is sure of the gospel of God's peace.

Lift up the shield of faith. No small matter in size or importance, this wooden shield was four feet tall and two and a half feet wide. It would protect the soldier's entire body, and it was especially important protection from the fiery arrows of the enemy, darts dipped in tar or pitch, set ablaze, and launched by the foe. A soldier whose shield was ablaze with fiery arrows might be tempted to drop his shield, his protection, and then would be vulnerable to spear or sword. But Roman soldiers covered their shields with thick leather and soaked their shields in water before battle so the fire of the enemy's arrows would be quickly quenched and nothing would cost them the protection of their shields. For God's people, our best and surest shield against any arrow of pain or temptation, heartache or suffering, is the shield of our faith in the God who has promised, "Never will I leave you; never will I forsake you."[7]

And now, dear soldier of faith's realm, you are almost ready for battle.

But, quickly now, to one knee! Bow in awe at the unexpected entrance of Heaven's High King!

You see, the last two items you'll need are gifts of grace straight from the hands of the Almighty to his soldier of faith.

Gifts of grace straight to you.

And they can be given by none other than Heaven's King.

In your left hand is your shield, but with your right hand reach out to accept the shining helmet freely extended and offered to you by Heaven's hand. It's the helmet of salvation.

There. Though you feel unworthy—and though apart from the love of the Prince of Peace, you are—feel, along with the gentle pressure of the burnished bronze helm now resting above your brow, the wonderfully liberating weight of the love and affirmation of Heaven itself.

And now, resting in the hands of the King whose hands fashioned all of creation and who once split the sky with Eternity's blade to grant glorious entrance to Heaven's advancing host, a sword. He stands and raises it high, whispers a word of promise and covenant and love, and slowly lowers the blade until it rests on first one of your trembling shoulders and then the other. He withdraws its blade, but extends his own deepest blessing, and then slowly but with no hint of doubt or trepidation extends the hilt toward you.

Take the sword. It is the very word of God. And you, mighty soldier of faith, have just received your commission from the King.

How to Measure a Rainbow

In that knowledge, stand fast, and "when the day of evil comes," know assuredly that you will indeed be able to stand your ground.

You are a soldier of the King!

I know. By yourself, you're a lot like me. Not all that daunting.

But you're not by yourself. Not any longer.

Because you're wearing Heaven's armor and marching in the service of Heaven's King, you can know that the battle is won and the victory is sure.

Maybe you've never felt like much of a soldier.

Maybe you've felt more like a Gomer Pyle than a Douglas MacArthur.

More like a buck private than a five-star General Eisenhower.

More like a raw recruit than a General Norman Schwartzkopf or a General Colin Powell.

I know how you feel.

I don't know much about being a soldier in our nation's military.

And I wonder myself sometimes about how much I really know about being a soldier in Christ's kingdom.

But I do know that most of the truly important lessons I've learned about being Christ's warrior, I learned from a far greater warrior than I, my father. Sometimes when you're just starting a journey, just beginning a tour of duty, just reflecting on a call and a commission, it helps to learn some lessons from the old veterans who've gone before. And sometimes you learn a lot from the way they finish their service.

My father's tour of duty just recently finished.

My family and I gathered with many we love to mark its end—and what we firmly believe was an even grander beginning as he was commissioned to a much loftier Post.

In this chapter, you and I have focused a bit on both ancient warriors and more modern soldiers. But if I had to pick a period to use to talk about a warrior like my father, I think I'd pick medieval times. Yes, I'm sure I would.

For our family, and for many we love, it was like Camelot, the mythical center of fabled King Arthur's Britain and all of his wonderful and legendary tales.

Yes, for us it was Camelot.

We were gathered for the funeral of my father, gathered through the kindness and generosity of the president of Abilene Christian University, Dad's alma mater, in the beautiful chapel of the university's College of Biblical Studies.

Picture a tall, vaulted and arched edifice at the top of a broad series of many steps reminiscent of those leading up to our nation's Capitol building. Scraping the sky above it all, a tall "prayer tower" (whose top, I think, will never be finished until it boasts a cross, but is still magnificent).

Picture the interior of the high-ceilinged sanctuary with its raised platform and pulpit front and center, and the sanctuary sides lined, floor to ceiling, with richly-colored and textured stained glass. And at the very front, at the culmination of the center aisle, on this day, and for the first time in this building's history, there rested a casket in the place of honor.

The scene felt right.

It *was* right.

It was just as it should have been.

In 1935, my father went out from this school having been graduated with highest honors. He went out to preach and to teach and to work for God's Kingdom, and though he didn't know it at the time, to spend a lifetime teaching others to preach and to labor in the service of the King.

How to Measure a Rainbow

And now we were back, marking the end of his full life and ministry. Full circle.

Back to the Round Table.

Back to Camelot.

I don't suppose that Dad ever thought of himself as a knight of high order. But from our little group of churches, our very small segment of the vastly larger Kingdom, many of our best, our noblest, our mightiest men (and women), several hundred in Abilene and 500-600 later in another memorial service in Houston, gathered to celebrate the coming home of this one who trained and loved and ministered to so many of them. Knights, so to speak, of the High King themselves, they gathered around this knight, the mentor and teacher of so many, and doffed their helmets in honor of one who fought only against evil and lived to proclaim the message of the High King.

A poet's words ascended into the air of the stained glass-hued Great Hall like doves of peace rising to circle in tribute, and the echo of every syllable reverberated in the hall, the soft wing-whispers of words given flight. They mingled in the air to give voice to a Christian knight's prayer to his Lord before meeting the last battle, the battle with death:

> When the night grows darkest,
> And the stars are pale,
> When the foe-men gather
> In death's misty vale,
> Be Thou Sword and Buckler,
> Be Thou Shield and Mail.[8]

"So no fears shall chill" the knight on "that unknown shore," the assurance of victory comes from the very Christ who "in death . . . conquered, / And can die no more."

It fell my lot to stand before the assembled company and to sing those words.

A Terminator, Too

It was one of the hardest things I have ever done.

It was one of the greatest privileges I have ever been granted.

I sang in honor of the father whose love and whose life led me to the best Father of all.

I sang the tribute of our family to the one, and to the One, who has pointed us to Heaven's best blessings.

I sang, and on the final verse, all those assembled to pay tribute joined me in praise to God:

Blessed warfare over,
Endless rest alone;*
Tears no more, nor sorrow,
Neither sigh nor moan,
But a song of triumph
Round about the throne.

       *only

And the notes of the song took wing to ascend in that beautiful chapel and, I'm convinced, to the Great Hall of Heaven, and for us it was Camelot indeed as we praised the High King for his mercy and his grace and for welcoming this faithful knight home.

My father was perhaps the kindest and gentlest, and at the same time, the strongest and most faithful, man I have ever known. In his life and in his death he conquered because he wore the colors of the King and faced all of his battles arrayed in the armor of the Kingdom.

There is a lesson in that for soldiers like you and like me.

And now, hold on, brace yourself, for a bit of a jarring shift of scene. Let's shift from Camelot to Cannon. (That's quite a trip!)

Cannon?

How to Measure a Rainbow

Yes, Cannon.

Cannon Air Force Base, Clovis, New Mexico.

Meet Chris Black.

Chris is a nice guy, a very capable young man. He graduated from high school in Ohio, and then went to Cornell University where he joined the Air Force ROTC and, upon graduation, went through pilot training in Mississippi. He not only earned his wings in the Magnolia state, he met Ellen, a beautiful Mississippi belle who has just become his wife (her father warned her about Air Force guys, but . . .), and they've moved to our town where Chris can drive west to the base and Ellen can drive east to law school.

And now it's been my family's privilege to share worship and the beginnings of friendship with Chris and Ellen.

The Blacks are a fine-looking and impressive couple. I think they both did very well indeed.

As you are meeting Chris right now, I'm sure you'll notice that he's a good looking guy. He seems strong and fit. He's obviously quite intelligent and well-spoken.

Did I mention that he's a soldier, an airman? Yes, I suppose I did, but you might have picked up some physical hints along that line anyway if you are really observant.

I'm sure Chris is well-trained physically and could hold his own quite well in a military fight. He's well-trained in every way and in great shape.

But let me tell you a secret. I don't think I'd put Chris up against Arnold Schwarzenegger in combat.

No, it just wouldn't be a fair fight.

Not fair at all.

Chris would beat the daylights out of Arnold.

Beat him.

Defeat him.

Utterly humiliate and destroy him.

A Terminator, Too

And I'd really hate to do that to Arnold.

The contest wouldn't even be close because, you see, when Chris puts on his armor, it's a G-suit, and he fights his battles strapped into the seat of a United States Air Force F-16 Falcon.

When Chris fights a battle, he fights it in a winged rocket capable of flying twice the speed of sound, withstanding nine times the force of gravity, all the while equipped with an amazingly diverse and deadly array of weapons, and rated as perhaps the most agile modern fighter aircraft in the world.

We ate lunch with Chris and Ellen at our church's fellowship meal on a recent Sunday. Chris and I talked about airplanes, and I mentioned how much I love to watch those jets fly, and I wondered if he might fly by a little closer to town sometime. (I also tried to help him with a problem he's had breaking up some concrete at his house. I did a little research and suggested either an AGM-65G Maverick air-to-ground missile or perhaps a GBU-15 Paveway TV-guided bomb. He seemed appreciative but thought the resulting hole might be a tad extreme.) On Monday, I heard what sounded like thunder, but I quickly recognized the mighty roar. I bailed out of the church office just in time to see two fine-looking F-16s scream by and bank magnificently. (If you need an air-strike called in sometime, just give me a call, and I'll see what I can do.)[9]

Now, do you see what I mean when I say that in a fight between Chris Black and Arnold Schwarzenegger, my money will be on Chris every time?

Arnold is a powerful figure. But compared to Chris and the weapon Chris wields and the authority that backs him up, Arnold suddenly seems a great deal less impressive.

If you need to go to war, be sure you've got the right armor. It makes all the difference.

If you need to go to war, be sure your weapons are the very weapons you need to do the job and to win.

If you need to go to war, make sure you've got the full weight and authority of a great kingdom backing your every blow.

Folks, we're at war.

And do you realize that the awesome power of an Air Force F-16 unleashed by the skill of a well-trained pilot and backed by the complete authority of the United States government is less than insignificant compared to the power of the omnipotent King we serve?

Let's put on the armor of God so that through his power we can stand our ground.

Let's use the weapons he promises will help us win.

Let's strike every blow under the full authority of the King.

Is the Enemy too strong for us?

Yes, by far!

But even he is no match for our King.

We serve, you see, the highest of High Kings,

   whose army will one day be forever victorious,

      whose Kingdom will never end,

         and whose name will forever be praised!

So, move over, Arnold Schwarzenegger, famed terminator of terminators. Under the authority of our King, God's people are terminators, too! But only Satan and his hosts need fear us.

All praise and glory to the High King of Heaven, the King we serve!

And "grace to all who love the Lord Jesus Christ with an undying love" (6:24)!

Notes

Chapter 1   "I Choose You!"

1. I should probably mention that I don't intend for one "brain-dead" coach to be an indictment of the breed. Some very fine friends, people who have been among God's best blessings to my family, have been coaches and former coaches of exactly the right sort. They're a credit to the profession. (I mean that sincerely. It's not just that I don't want to have to run laps for an unfortunate lapse of the tongue!)

2. Morris Mandel, *The Jewish Press*, as quoted in *Leadership Journal*, Winter 1985, 49.

3. Matthew 25:21, 40, author's paraphrase.

Chapter 2   "Enlightened Eyes"

1. Edith Schaeffer, A Way of Seeing (Tarrytown, New York: Fleming H. Revell Company, 1977).

2. Kenneth Barker, gen. ed., *The NIV Study Bible* (Grand Rapids, Michigan: Zondervan Bible Publishers, 1985), 1700. See also Acts 28:16, 30.

3. Viktor E. Frankl, *Man's Search for Meaning* (German, 1946; English, 1959; 4th. ed., Boston: Beacon Press, 1992), 118-19.

4.   Frankl, 119.

5.   Frankl, 119.

6.   Frankl, 109.

7.   Will Durant, *Caesar and Christ*, The Story of Civilization, vol. 3 (New York: Simon and Schuster, 1944), 90.

8.   The dialogue that follows is all based on 2 Kings 6, but, though some is exact, much is my *very* loose paraphrase.

Chapter 3   The Post Office, the Pharisees, and Lazarus

1.   I was right about this particular "prophecy," even though I have no crystal ball, I don't read tea leaves, and every organization I'm associated with is truly both non-profit and non-prophet. Since I first penned this chapter, we have indeed changed local postmasters. The new one is also a fine guy and a friend who works hard to be accommodating and efficient as do his employees who are some exceptionally nice people (and I'd very much like for them to remain my friends once this is published). One of them even went far past the second mile to help me the day I dropped a bank deposit envelope right into the hopper along with a wad of bills. Our local postal folks have done me many more kindnesses than that one and have kept me, more than once, from blundering blindly right into the sort of bureaucratic perdition that ends in total strangulation by red tape. I like our local folks, but the larger organization is still a bureaucracy by anybody's definition. Just take a peek at any of their forms.

2. Luke 11:46, as paraphrased by Eugene H. Peterson, *The Message* (Colorado Springs, Colorado: NavPress, 1993), 175.

3.   John 8:1-11.

4.   Matthew 23:15.

5.   In a work which is rightly termed a Christian classic, Hannah Whitall Smith says regarding the Christian life of faith that "man's part is to trust, and God's part is to work" (*The Christian's Secret of a Happy Life* [Old Tappan, New Jersey:

Fleming H. Revell Company, 1942; 33rd reprint, Spire Books, 1981, 21]). See Romans 12:1-2, 2 Corinthians 3:17-18, Ephesians 2:10, and (though this Scripture has often been twisted into a kind of "works" salvation Paul would not recognize) Philippians 2:12-13.

6. This is neither Scripture nor scriptural.

7. Ephesians 2:10, but twisted.

8. Read 1 John and you'll see clearly that this is not the way God intends his people to live, that God intends for his people to be secure in their salvation through Jesus Christ.

9. Charles Dickens, *A Christmas Carol* (Philadelphia: J. B. Lippincott Company, 1915 [first published in 1843]), 4.

10. The account that follows is from John 11. Some of the quotations are exact, but most are my loose paraphrase.

Chapter 4   A Hole in the Wall

1. Golda Meir, as quoted in "Reflections," *Christianity Today*, date unknown.

2. Leroy Garrett, *The Stone Campbell Movement* (Joplin, Missouri: College Press, 1981), 113, 496, 619, 670-80.

3. Garrison Keillor, *Leaving Home* (New York: Penguin Books, 1987), 161-66.

4. Keillor, 164.

5. Keillor, 164.

6. Keillor, 164-66.

7. Acts 10:1-48.

8. Acts 9:1-20.

9. F. F. Bruce, *Paul: Apostle of the Heart Set Free* (Grand Rapids, Michigan: William B. Eerdmans Publishing Company, 1977), 21.

10. Joe Maxwell, "Racial Healing in the Land of Lynching," *Christianity Today*, 10 January 1994, 24-26.

Chapter 5   Paint Creek & the Mystery of Christ

1.   More evidence of the conclusions being drawn here, my father's grave is now also there beside my mother's.

2.   Based on Exodus 2-3.

3.   Matthew 3:17, KJV.

4.   John 19:30.

5.   Luke 23:46, RSV.

6.   Matthew 28:6, PHILLIPS.

7.   Revelation 5:12.

8.   1 John 4:16.

Chapter 6   How To Measure a Rainbow

1. Alan Shepard and Deke Slayton, with Jay Barbree and Howard Benedict, *Moon Shot: The Inside Story of America's Race to the Moon* (Atlanta: Turner Publishing, Inc., 1994), 154-56. The "poetic" aspect of Carpenter's character is further expounded in the video based on the book (*Moon Shot*, VHS videocassette, dir. Kirk Wolfinger, narr. Barry Corbin, Turner Home Entertainment, 1994, cat. no. 3144, 189 minutes).

2.   Actually, Carpenter splashed down a "mere" 250 miles past his intended landing point (*Moon Shot*, 155); it was the crew of Gemini 8, Neil Armstrong and Dave Scott, who did indeed splash down "5,000 miles off course in the wrong ocean" (*Moon Shot* video) following a harrowing flight and a very close call. That they came back at all is a tribute to Armstrong's skill as a pilot.

3.   Matthew 27:46.

4.   Max Lucado, *The Great House of God* (Dallas: Word Publishing, 1997), 126.

5.   Not his real name. I'd prefer not to test his gracious disposition too severely.

6.   Lloyd John Ogilvie, *The Bush Is Still* Burning (Waco, Texas: Word Publishing, 1980), 23.

Chapter 7   Running on the Right Road

1. Eugene H. Peterson, *The Message* (Colorado Springs, Colorado: NavPress, 1993), 479.

2. G. Harvey, *The Blessing*, a painting commissioned by Focus on the Family, December 1998.

3. *The Message*, 480.

4. Paul Brand and Philip Yancey, *Fearfully and Wonderfully Made* (Grand Rapids, Michigan: Zondervan Publishing, 1980), 5.

5. Brand and Yancey, 46.

6. Brand and Yancey, 44-45.

7. Brand and Yancey, 45.

8. Brand and Yancey, 47.

9. *The Message*, 479.

10. Natalie Sleeth, "Hymn of Promise" (Hope Publishing, 1986).

11. *The Message*, 480.

Chapter 8   A Dragon's Tale

1. C. S. Lewis, *The Chronicles of Narnia* (1950-1956; New York: Collier Books, 1970), and J. R. R. Tolkien, *The Lord of the Rings* (New York: Ballantine Books edition, 1965).

2. C. S. Lewis, *The Last Battle* (New York: Collier Books, 1956), 172-184.

3. C. S. Lewis, *The Voyage of the Dawn Treader* (New York: Collier Books, 1952), 1.

4. *The Message*, 480.

5. Paul Harvey, as quoted in *Leadership Journal*, Winter 1987, 41.

6. Stephen R. Donaldson, *The Chronicles of Thomas Covenant* (New York: Ballantine Books, 1977), and The Second Chronicles of Thomas Covenant (New York: Ballantine Books, 1980-1983).

7. "Leprosy," *Microsoft Encarta 98 Encyclopedia* (1993-1997).

8. "Leprosy," *Microsoft Encarta 98*.

9. Stephen R. Donaldson, *Lord Foul's Bane* (New York: Ballantine Books, 1977), 14.

10. "Leprosy," *Microsoft Encarta 98*.

11. Donaldson, 2.

12. Paul Brand and Philip Yancey, *In His Image* (Grand Rapids, Michigan: Zondervan Publishing, 1984; paperback, 1987), 239-41.

13. Covenant's wife seems to be correct when she says that most people who acquire the disease were exposed to it as children, but it still is only very minimally contagious even to kids (Donaldson, 13, 18).

14. Donaldson, 15.

15. *The Voyage of the Dawn Treader*, 90-91.

Chapter 9   Living a Life of Love

1. Paul O'Donnell et al., "Like Candy From an Heiress," *Newsweek* (8 Aug. 1994): 60.

2. Bailey was involved enough that in March 1995 he pleaded guilty to fraud, racketeering, and other crimes for which the combined sentences totaled up to 150 years (*The Washington Post*, March 2, 1995, p. A8, and Animal People World Wide Web site, "Court Calendar," April 1995).

3. Keith Miller, *The Taste of New Wine*, new ed. (Waco, Texas: Word Books, 1979), 30.

4. *The Message*, 481.

5. John Drescher, *If I Were Starting My Family Again* (Intercourse, Pennsylvania: Good Books, 1994), 55.

6. The form of this poem, though not its content, is based on Stephen R. Donaldson's poem in *Lord Foul's Bane*, 147.

Chapter 10   To Live in the Light

1. *Indiana Jones and the Last Crusade*, VHS videocassette, dir. Steven Spielberg, Paramount, 1989, 128 minutes.

2. John V. Halvorson, *Is There a Word?* (Decorah, Iowa: Anundsen Publishing, 1988), 53.

3. I love the words Michael Card penned for his lilting and beautiful Celtic song "Starkindler":

> *A billion bright and holy beams*
> *From a light that's traveled far*
> *Began the trip from His fingertips—*
> *O the wonder of the stars!—*
> *Proclaim the signs and seasons*
> *So silently they sing*
> *Of the wonder of their Kindler*
> *Of the power of their King.*
>
> *O the fiery suns above us*
> *In the vast veil of the sky*
> *Are Your servant flames of fire,*
> *Are Your silent holy guides,*
> *And like the star-led magi*
> *They guide our souls to You*
> *And shine a light of awesome love*
> *Into eyes that see anew.*

Michael Card, *Starkindler*, (music, Michael Card with Planxly Garvin), Mole End Music, 1998.

4. *The Message*, 481.

5. *The Message*, 481-82.

6. Halvorson, 53-55.

7. Andrew T. Lincoln, *Ephesians*, ed. David Hubbard et al., Word Biblical Commentary, vol. 42 (Dallas, Texas: Word Publishing, 1990), 335.

8. "Death," in "To Illustrate," *Leadership Journal*, Spring 1998, 73.

Chapter 11　When You're Walking in Dangerous Territory

1. C. S. Lewis, *Mere Christianity* (New York: Macmillan Publishing Company, 1943), 51.
2. *Mere Christianity*, 51.
3. Amy Grant, words, and Michael W. Smith, music, "Thy Word" (Nashville, Tennessee: Bug and Bear Music, 1984).
4. "This World Is Not My Home," traditional spiritual.
5. *The Last Battle*, 169.
6. *The Last Battle*, 171.
7. *Mere Christianity*, 51.

Chapter 12　The Servant King

1. John 13:1-17.
2. Luke 7:36-50.
3. Luke 22:24. See also Luke 9:46 and Mark 9:34.
4. *The Message*, 171.
5. Matthew 18:21, author's paraphrase.
6. Matthew 18:22, PHILLIPS.
7. *The NIV Study Bible*, 1468.
8. Luke 12:13, author's paraphrase.
9. *The Message*, 177.
10. *The Message*, 482.
11. *The NIV Study Bible*, 1798.
12. *The Message*, 482.
13. By the way, the genuine forgiveness that God extends to us and that Christ requires us to extend to others is never given to enable wrong and hurtful behavior. It is given to enable healing.
14. *The NIV Study Bible*, 1798.

Chapter 13   A Terminator, Too!

1.   This is not a film recommendation, but since I allude to the movies a few times, I should give appropriate credit for: *The Terminator*, VHS videocassette, dir. James Cameron, Artisan Entertainment, 1984, 108 minutes; and *Terminator 2: Judgment Day*, VHS videocassette, dir. James Cameron, Artisan Entertainment, 1991, 139 minutes.

2.   Luci Shaw, "Mary's Song," Christianity Today, 14 December 1984, 18. [Reprinted in *Christianity Today* from *A Widening Light: Poems of the Incarnation*, ed. Luci Shaw (Wheaton, Illinois: Harold Shaw Publishers, 1984).]

3.   Luke 2:25-38.

4.   Matthew 11:1-6 and Luke 7:18-23.

5.   For the description of the Christian's armor, and for several observations and comments in this paragraph and the following paragraphs in this section dealing with this subject, I have drawn significantly upon the previously noted work of Andrew T. Lincoln, *Ephesians*, 429-60.

6.   Isaiah 52:7

7.   Hebrews 13:5b, and see Deuteronomy 31:6, 8.

8.   The words of this and the verses that follow are from the beautiful hymn "When Days Shadows Lengthen," words by F. G. Lee; traditional melody, arr. Nicola Montani, copyright 1920 by N. A. Montani, printed in *Great Songs of the Church, Number Two*, 45th ed. (Chicago: Great Songs Press, 1973), hymn no. 531.

9.   If you've got concrete of your own to knock out, I'd suggest renting a jackhammer. But if you want to research the F-16 option, I'd suggest the same web sites where I found my information: "The F-16 Fighting Falcon" USAF Fact Sheet (http://www.af.mil/news/factsheets/F_16_Fighting_Falcon.html) , "The F-16 Page" (http://www.geocities.com/CapeCanaveral/ 6106/), and "General Dynamics F-16 Fighting Falcon"

About the Author

urtis K. Shelburne was born and raised in Amarillo, Texas. The son of a minister and the brother of three ministers curtis graduated from Tascosa High School and later san Jacinto college, Abilene Christian University, and West Texas A & M University. He holds a B.A. degree in Bible and a MA degree in English Literature. He has served churches in Houston, Amarillo and Odessa, And has been for the past fourteen years the minister of the 16th and D Church of Christ in Muleshoe. Curtis writes a weekly newspaper column, *Focus on Faith*, and has served for fifteen years as the Managing Editor for *The Christian Appeal*, a monthly devotional magazine.

Curtis is in his fifth term on the Muleshoe Independent School District Board of Trustees where he has served for twelve years and now serves as vice president—a board, by the way, honored several years ago by the Texas Association of School Boards as one of the five honored boards among the 1000 or so boards in the State of Texas. He is a former Chairman of the Visiting Committee for the English Department of Abilene Christian University, having served four years in that committee and is a Dean of the Summer Excitement youth leadership school which is held each summer on the campus of dallas Christian College. Frequently speaking at community events and serving as a guest motivational speaker at churches, schools, and other organizations in Texas, New Mexico, Arizona, and Indiana. Curtis also enjoy singing and has sung with the Psalms IV Quartet, the Singing Men of West Texas, and has recently appeared in the role of John Masters for the Muleplex Production Company's outdoor drama, *Keepers of the Legend*

His most important accolade by far, he says, comes as the husband of Juana and the father of four sons, Christopher, Jeffrey, Stephan, and Joshua.

The most effective leadership, Curtis believes, is that patterned after the Father of us all who has blessed us with the gift of life and filled our lives with joy for the journey.